Royal Exchange Theatre and Pingng Productions present

CROCODILES

by Lee Mattinson

Winner of the Royal Exchange Theatre Hodgkiss Award

PINGNg

1–18 October 2014
Royal Exchange Theatre, Manchester

CROCODILES

by Lee Mattinson

CORNELIA GLASS	Melanie Hill
VINCENT GLASS	James Atherton
RUDOLPH GLASS	Kevin Wathen
MATILDA GLASS	Sarah Gordy

Director	Ng Choon Ping
Designer	Sarah Beaton
Lighting Designer	Matthew Haskins
Sound Designer	Dominic Kennedy
Video Designer	Gillian Tan
Fight Director	Bret Yount
Assistant Director	Charlotte Lewis
Production Manager	Helen C Gorton
Casting Director	Jerry Knight-Smith CDG

Stage Manager	Philip Hussey
Deputy Stage Manager	Bobbi McGlade

For PINGNG Productions

Director	Ng Choon Ping
Producer	Gillian Tan
Associate Producer	Hon Jia Xuan
Associate Producer	Mary Halton
Digital Design	Moira Lam

THE COMPANY

JAMES ATHERTON (Vincent Glass) is making his first appearance for the Royal Exchange Theatre. Other theatre includes: *Wallenstein* (Chichester Festival); *Treasure Island* (West End). Television credits include: *Hollyoaks Late Night*, *Hollyoaks* (series regular); *Inspector George Gently*, *Joe Maddison's War*, *Doctors* and *Casualty 1909*.

SARAH GORDY (Matilda Glass) is making her first appearance for the Royal Exchange Theatre. Other theatre includes: *Into the Blue* (Arcola); *When We Were Mothers* (Orange Tree, Richmond/New Victoria); *Seize the Day* (Hijinx) and *Walking On Water* (Theatre Centre). Television credits include: *Call the Midwife*, *Holby City*, *Upstairs Downstairs* (series regular), *Doctors*, *Casualty* and *Peak Practice*.

MELANIE HILL (Cornelia Glass) has previously appeared at the Royal Exchange Theatre in *I Have Been Here Before*. Other theatre includes: *Nativities*, *Inheritance* (Live Theatre Company); *Maggie's End* (Shaw); *Tongue of a Bird* (Almeida); *Cardiff East* (National Theatre); *Bread* (Dominion); *Women Beware Women* (Royal Court); *Fire in the Lake, Who Killed Hilda Murrell* (Newcastle Playhouse); *Breezeblock Park, Dirty Linen, Deathtrap, Twelfth Night, Selfish Shellfish* (Redgrave, Farnham); *Educating Rita* (British American Theatre). Television credits include: *Hebburn*, *Waterloo Road* (series regular), *Merlin*, *The Body Farm*, *Candy Cabs* (series regular), *Joe Maddison's War*, *The Thick of It*, *Holby City*, *Rather You Than Me*, *White Girl*, *The Street*, *Cape Wrath* (series regular), *Emmerdale* (semi-regular), *The Brief*, *The Fugitives* (series regular), *The Singing Cactus*, *The Bill* (semi-regular), *Hot Money*, *NCS Manhunt* (series regular), *Close and True*, *Silent Witness*, *Playing the Field* (series regular), *The Widowing of Mrs Holroyd*, *Crocodile Shoes* (series regular), *The Beast in Man, Finney* (series regular), *Circles Of Deceit: Dark Secret, Cardiac Arrest* (series regular), *Casualty, Spender, Bread* (series regular), *Boon, A Night on the Tyne*, *Juliet Bravo* and *Auf Wiedersehen Pet* (series regular). Film credits include: *Unconditional, Stardust, United, From Hell, Brassed Off, When Saturday Comes, Shopping* and *The Hawk*. Radio includes: *Black Roses: The Trial*.

KEVIN WATHEN (Rudolph Glass) is making his first appearance for the Royal Exchange Theatre. Other theatre credits include: *Billy Elliot* (Victoria Palace Theatre); *Quadrophenia* (Plymouth Theatre Royal/national tour); *Breakfast with Johnny Wilkinson* (Menier Chocolate Factory); *Hair* (Gate); *Alice's Adventures in Wonderland* (Bristol Old Vic); *Hamlet* (Old Vic); *Skellig* (Young Vic). Television credits include: *Doctors, Inspector George Gently, Blue Murder, Holby City, Silent Witness, The Bill* and *Judge John Deed*. Film credits include: *Care* and *And Kill Them*.

NG CHOON PING (Director) graduated from York University and Central School of Speech and Drama. Directing credits include *Snap* (Young Vic); *Golden Child* (New Diorama); *Armed Forces Day* (Riverside Studios) and *Pure O* (King's Head Theatre). Assistant directing credits include *Chimerica* (Almeida/West End); *nut* (National Theatre) and *Bakersfield Mist* (West End). He was text associate at the Shakespeare's Globe and is a founding director of Pingng Productions.

LEE MATTINSON (Writer) Lee graduated from Northumbria University with a BA in Fine Art and is co-artistic director of Chicken Pox Fox Productions. Theatre credits include: *Brown Bird* (Chicken Pox Fox); *Snap* (Young Vic); *Gary Lineker is Gay* (Paines Plough); Geisha Girls (Bush); *Chalet Lines* (Bush/Live); *No Wire Hangers* (Soho); *Lashes and Taches* (Arts in Touch); *Donna Disco* (Chicken Pox Fox/Live); *Lamb* (Dot-to-Dot Active Arts); *Me and Cilla, M&S S&M, Orlando Spoon, Julian Scary, I Heart Morrissey, Liquorice, Shitty Shitty Bang Bang, 6c Nativity, Circus Girl* (Live); *Jonathan Likes This* (National Theatre/Live); *Swan Song* (New Writing North); *I Heart Catherine Pistachio, The Streets in the Sky, Choir* (Encounter); *Never Forget* (Queen's Hall); *Chocolate* (West Yorkshire Playhouse); *LOL* (East 15); *Colour It In, Rola Cola, Freddy Hearts Freddie, Me Fatty* (Ugly Sister); *The Bang Gang* (Bad Fox/NTC); *Rabbit Rabbit Rabbit* (NTC); *Paper Men Hold Hands* (Monster Productions); *Monster* (Bold as Brass). Radio credits include: *Me and Cilla, Glow in the Dark* (BBC Radio 3); *Magpie* (BBC Radio 4); *Prom, Snowglobe* (BBC Radio Newcastle). TV credits include: *Coronation Street* (Story Associate, ITV); *Scallywagga* (BBC3). Film credits include: *Harvest* (Superkrush Films); *Take My Bones* (SiZe Records).

SARAH BEATON (Designer) Sarah is a UK based performance designer. She studied Design for Stage at the Royal Central School of Speech and Drama, graduating in 2011 with First Class Honours. Sarah was awarded The Linbury Prize for Stage Design. She was nominated for the Arts Foundation Fellowship 2013 by Katrina Lindsay and was selected to exhibit her work at World Stage Design 2013 in Cardiff. She has a particular interest in working within an ensemble.

DOMINIC KENNEDY (Sound Designer) Dominic Kennedy is a sound designer and composer for performance and live events. He has a keen interest in developing new work and implementing sound design from an early stage in the theatre making process. Dominic is a graduate from Central School of Speech and Drama where he developed specialist skills in collaborative and devised theatre making, music composition and installation practices. Dominic has recently designed shows and collaborated with Paines Plough, Choon Ping, Song Theatre, Jamie Wood, Gameshow, Engineer, Outbox, Jemima James and Mars Tarrab. Dominic recently was associate sound designer with Pete Malkin on *War Correspondents*. He was also associate designer with Tom Gibbons for the Paines Ploughs Roundabout touring season 2014. Recent installation work includes interactive sound design for Gingerline a pop-up restaurant and art space.

MATTHEW HASKINS (Lighting Designer) Theatre credits include: *A Bright Room Called Day* (Southwark Playhouse); *1001 Nights* (Unicorn/New Wolsey); *Wind in the Willows, The Years Between* (Royal & Derngate); *truth and reconciliation* (Royal Court); *Dream Story, Mud* (Gate); *The Picture of John Gray* (Old Red Lion); *Steel Magnolias* (David Ian Productions – Bath Theatre Royal/ UK tour); *How to be Immortal* (UK tour); *Bandages* (UK tour). Opera credits include: *La Traviata, Don Giovanni, Turn of the Screw, Cautionary Tales* (Opera North); *The Commission, Cafe Kafka* (Royal Opera House/Aldeburgh Music/ Opera North); *Anna Bolena, Roberto Devereux, Maria Stuarda* (Welsh National Opera); *Maria Stuarda* (Royal Opera House Oman); *Turn of the Screw* (The Israeli Opera); *Babur in London* (The Opera Group); *Into the Little Hill* (Hamburg Laeiszhalle); *La Cenerentola* (Malmö Opera). Site Specific projects include: *Walk With Me* (Girl Effect/Punchdrunk); *Open Outcry* (Barclays); Elle Style Awards 2014, *Havana 7 Days, Thanks a Million, Cabaret Les Embiez* and other numerous projects (Blonstein & Associates); Universal Brits Party (Soho House); *Dido Queen of Carthage* (Kensington Palace); *Sea Tongue* (The Shout); *Encounters* (Greenwich & Docklands Festival). Other and associate credits include: *The Master and Margarita, Shun-Kin, A Disappearing Number* (Complicite); *Grace Jones* (Royal Albert Hall).

GILLIAN TAN (Video Designer) Gillian Tan is a Visual Engineer and Specialist Producer, exploring the use of projection and video in the entertainment industry through the development of new technologies, as well as challenging the boundaries of audience experiences in live events and theatre. Recent credits include: Associate Video Designer for Wizard Production's *I Believe In Unicorns* at the Vaudeville Theatre (West End); Video Engineer for Secret Cinema's *Back To The Future*; Digital Engineer for Brolly Production's workshop of *Clocks, The Steampunk Opera*; Associate Producer for The McOnie Company's *Drunk*. She would like to thank Tim Bird and Lucy Ockenden for their unwavering support, the Royal Exchange Theatre for this opportunity and Ng Choon Ping for always believing.

CHARLOTTE LEWIS (Assistant Director) is currently a student on the MA Theatre Directing course at Birkbeck University of London. This is her first show with The Royal Exchange Theatre. Her recent work includes working with Gabrielle Reidy on *The Seven Pomegranate Seeds* by Colin Teevan and a showing of Rebecca Hill's *Torque* at The Ovalhouse theatre in London.

Situated in the heart of Manchester the Royal Exchange is one of the UK's leading producing theatres and is home to two performance spaces – a 750-seat glass and steel in-the-round theatre and a 100-seat flexible studio space. The Company's own productions appear alongside a diverse touring programme of work.

The Royal Exchange nurtures outstanding creative talent in Manchester and attracts some of the most original artists and theatre makers in the country to present high-quality classic plays and new writing to entertain, provoke and inspire.

The Company is committed to supporting and developing new writing. It runs the bi-annual Bruntwood Prize for Playwriting – the UK's biggest playwriting competition. *Crocodiles* will be the fifth world premiere presented by the Royal Exchange in 2014 – following *Blindsided* by Simon Stephens, *Pests* by Vivienne Franzmann, *The Last Days of Troy* by Simon Armitage and *Britannia Waves the Rules* by Gareth Farr.

Crocodiles by Lee Mattinson is the winner of the inaugural Royal Exchange Theatre Hodgkiss Award, which celebrates the unique collaboration between a writer and a director. The Royal Exchange is grateful to Sue Hodgkiss CBE whose support has made the Hodgkiss Award possible.

The Great Hall of the Royal Exchange

Royal Exchange Theatre, St. Ann's Square, Manchester, M2 7DH
www.royalexchange.co.uk +44 161 833 9833

Registered Charity Number 255424

ROYAL EXCHANGE THEATRE STAFF

OUR SUPPORTERS

MAJOR SPONSORS

bruntwood ●

 manchester airport

thistle
MANCHESTER THE PORTLAND

PROJECT SUPPORTERS

The Andrew Lloyd Webber
  Foundation
The Austin and Hope
  Pilkington Trust
The BBC Performing Arts
  Fund
Blitz Communications
Boshier-Hinton Foundation
Cargill Plc
The John S Cohen Foundation
Ernest Cook Trust
The Co-operative Foundation
Computeam
The Noël Coward Foundation
The Duchy of Lancaster
  Charitable Trust
Garfield Weston Foundation
The Garrick Charitable Trust
The Gladys Jones Charitable
  Trust
The Granada Foundation
The J Paul Getty Jnr
  Charitable Trust
The J S F Pollitzer Charitable
  Trust
John Thaw Foundation
The Madeline Mabey Trust
Manchester Guardian Society
  Charitable Trust
The Mills and Reeve
  Charitable Trust
The Oglesby Charitable Trust
The Peter Henriques
  Memorial Fund
PricewaterhouseCoopers
The Rayne Foundation
Schroder Charitable Trust
Enid Slater Charitable Trust
Susan Hodgkiss
Transport for Greater
  Manchester

PRINCIPAL MEMBERSHIP

Bruntwood
CISCO
Edmundson Electrical Ltd
Manchester Airport
Regatta

ENCORE MEMBERSHIP

Cityco
Dewhurst Torevell
DWF
Eckersley Entertainment
Fido PR
Greater Manchester Chamber
  of Commerce
Pricewaterhouse Coopers
Thistle Manchester City
  Centre – The Portland

ASSOCIATE MEMBERSHIP

Acies Group LLP
Atticus Legal LLP
Baker Tilly
Beaverbrooks
Cargill Plc
Crowe Clark Whitehill
DLA Piper UK
Galloways Printers
Heatons LLP
HFL Building Solutions
Grant Thornton
Hollins Strategic Land
The Midland Hotel
Manchester Law Society
Mohindra Maini LLP Solicitors
Sanderson Weatherall LLP
Smart Alex
Tangerine PR
Whitebirk Finance

PLATINUM MEMBERSHIP

Chris & Sue Bangs
Angela Brookes
Professor R A Burchell
Annabel & James Carter
John & Penny Early
Peter & Judy Folkman
Robin & Mary Taylor
David & Susan Walter
Helen & Phil Wile

EXCHANGE SUITE SUPPORTERS

5plus Architects – Interior
  Design Partner
Paint kindly provided by
  Farrow & Ball
Light fittings by Litecraft
Carpet by Shaw Contract
  Group

PATRONS £1000+ pa

Arnold and Brenda Bradshaw
Maureen Casket
Meg Cooper
Nick & Lesley Hopkinson

Dr and Mrs Elaine Johnson
Shirley Murtagh
Stephen and Judy Poster
Martin and Sandra Stone

CATALYST DONORS

Anonymous
Roy Beckett
Sir Robert & Mrs Meriel Boyd
Bernard & Julia De Sousa
John & Penny Early
The Friends
Martin Harrison &
  Frances Hendrix
Eve & Peter Keeling
Chris & Mike Potter
Dr J L Pearsall
Jennifer Raffle
Martyn & Valerie Torevell
Gerry & Joanne Yeung

REGULAR GIVING MEMBERS GOLD MEMBERSHIP £240+ pa

Mr D Ainsworth
G W Ball
Mr & Mrs Bradshaw
Gary Buttriss-Holt
Mr P J Craven
Mr Peter Cooper
P J Duke
Mrs Valerie Dunne
Rosalind Emsley-Smith
Mrs V Fletcher
Mr G J Garbett
Howard Gilby
Irene Gray
Mrs L Hawkins
George Ian Hood
Andrew Horner
Austen Livesy
Amina Latimer
Gillian & Kieron Lonergan
Marion Elizabeth Mackay
Jon Mason
Mr Donald Mather
Mr & Mrs Meldrum
Helen McPherson
Mr G M Morton
Pannone LLP
Ms Elizabeth Redmond
Mr & Mrs Rose
Emma Sheldon
Sandra Thomas
Miss G B Turner
Ian Warren
Mr J D Wignall

For a full list of Silver
Membership supporters
please visit
royalexchange.co.uk/donors

CROCODILES

Lee Mattinson

To my brothers, Simon and Steven

Characters

CORNELIA GLASS, *the mother, fifty-two*
VINCENT GLASS, *the younger son, thirty*
RUDOLPH GLASS, *the older son, thirty-five*
MATILDA GLASS, *the wife, thirty-seven*

This text went to press before the end of rehearsals and so may differ slightly from the play as performed.

Scene One

A derelict seaside town somewhere in the North of England.

Lights up on the front room of a once-lavish guesthouse.

Downstage left is a bay window, upstage left a dining table and washing machine, downstage right is a sofa and fridge, upstage centre the door to the main entrance hall.

The curtains are vile, the carpet stained, the chandelier cobwebbed.

The wall upstage right has been haphazardly demolished to reveal a kitchen, cooker and sink, set back from the main space. The breach in the wall has been integrated into everyday life despite the mess of rubble, peeling wallpaper, light switches spiralling out from the wall. A serving hatch remains.

CORNELIA *is sat on the sofa, knitting.*

Enter MATILDA *from the kitchen carrying a plate of French Fancies, a bowl of Skips, across the next section creating a buffet on the dining table.*

CORNELIA. Make sure to pop the brown Fondant Fancies to the front, they're always the last to go.

MATILDA. They're French Fancies.

CORNELIA. I couldn't give a shit if they're turning Japanese en route, just whack them at the front.

MATILDA. Will I put some cherryade out?

CORNELIA. Christ, no, crack open that cream soda we keep in the garage for good and, if there's four or more Moomin napkins knocking about from our Lucy's christening, dot a few of them about, too.

MATILDA. I don't think there is.

CORNELIA. Well, have a look, anyhow.

MATILDA. They're in the loft.

CORNELIA. The exercise'll do you good.

MATILDA. I'll just finish this.

CORNELIA (*mocking*). 'I'll just finish this' –

Enter RUDOLPH.

You'll never fathom what's happened, Rudolph, never in a month of Sundays.

RUDOLPH. Is the immersion on?

CORNELIA. Vincent's come home. He's come back to us.

RUDOLPH. Vincent?

CORNELIA. The one and the only, Rudolph.

RUDOLPH. What's he said?

CORNELIA. Not much, just landed half an hour back. He's up there now splashing his pits, said the ferry over was ninety-nine per cent foreigners.

RUDOLPH. It's about time he showed his face.

CORNELIA. He's saying he's only staying a few days. But I'm sure, once we get our claws in, we can lengthen it to a whole week of wonder.

RUDOLPH. Because he's nowhere else to go?

CORNELIA. Because this is his rightful home. He'll tell us when he's good and ready.

MATILDA. Has he definitely been fired?

CORNELIA. That new presenter's not a patch on him.

RUDOLPH. He might want to tell us –

CORNELIA (*snaps*). I won't have you forcing the issue, Rudolph.

I mean it. Do not make me sit you on that naughty step. And that goes for you, too, Matilda.

MATILDA. I won't. I promise.

CORNELIA. Rudolph?

RUDOLPH. Promise.

MATILDA. He's lovely.

CORNELIA. She'd never even met him.

'Who's this?' he says. We were in kinks, weren't we, Matilda? I had to have a sit-down, she almost bloody fainted.

MATILDA. You can tell he's not from round here.

RUDOLPH. He is from round here.

CORNELIA. What your wife's trying to say, is there's a touch of class to him.

RUDOLPH *points at the buffet.*

RUDOLPH. This isn't for him?

CORNELIA. Smelt like a small regional branch of the Body Shop, didn't he, Matilda?

MATILDA. White Musk.

CORNELIA. White Musk, Rudolph. My nose'll never be as lucky again.

Look at him, Matilda. Shell shocked and rightly so. I was the same, cat with my tongue and heart in my mouth.

MATILDA (*to* RUDOLPH). How was your matinee?

CORNELIA. Quiet, Matilda –

CORNELIA *listens at the door.*

He's here, I can hear him, stand in a line like the von Trapps –

RUDOLPH *and* MATILDA *line up in front of the sofa.*

Enter VINCENT, *stands in the doorway.*

CORNELIA *beams, proud as punch, poised for something almighty to happen. It doesn't.*

Well, say something, someone.

VINCENT. Can anyone else smell crab?

CORNELIA. That's him.

RUDOLPH. Sorry.

CORNELIA. You're being rude, Rudolph, say 'hello'.

RUDOLPH. Hello, Vincent.

VINCENT. Hiya, Rudolph.

CORNELIA. Hug each other. (*To* MATILDA.) They look like a cat staring at itself in a mirror –

VINCENT *and* RUDOLPH *reluctantly hug*.

Matilda?

MATILDA. Can I interest you in a French Fancy, Vincent?

CORNELIA. Give him some air, for Christ's sake – (*To* VINCENT.) here –

CORNELIA *hugs* VINCENT, *squeezes him like he's going out of fashion*.

My beautiful boy. (*To* RUDOLPH.) Get him a cream soda out the garage. (*To* VINCENT.) You do still like cream soda, don't you, Vincent?

VINCENT. Course.

CORNELIA. Course he does, Rudolph, quick as your little legs'll carry you.

Exit RUDOLPH.

VINCENT. What happened to your kitchen?

CORNELIA. We're going for open-plan, aren't we, Matilda? Saw it in a magazine, thought 'I'm having that'.

VINCENT. Which magazine?

CORNELIA. *Good Food Magazine*, they give them away for free in the dentist's.

MATILDA. They had a quiche in theirs.

CORNELIA. I says, you can keep the quiche.

VINCENT. It's lush.

CORNELIA. It is lush. It is. Yes.

Do you fancy a Fancy?

VINCENT. I'm fine.

CORNELIA. Sit down, then. Just here next to me, that's it. That's my brave boy. My beautiful, back-by-my-side and blistering boy.

CORNELIA *pulls* VINCENT *across to the sofa, sits him down next to her.*

Enter RUDOLPH *with a bottle of cream soda.*

RUDOLPH. Does everyone want some of this?

CORNELIA (*to* VINCENT). You'll've noticed Rudolph's still four foxes short of a fur coat.

(*To* RUDOLPH, *patronising.*) Course we do, Rudolph, there's a fistful of beakers on the draining board.

(*To* VINCENT.) I can hardly believe it's you. That you're here and home again. I'd pinch myself but I bruise very easily these days, Vincent.

CORNELIA *reaches into her knitting bag, pulls out a jumper.*

I knitted you this for this very eventuality.

CORNELIA *holds it up against* VINCENT, *it has a smiling sun up the front but would never fit him, it's child-sized.*

It has been a while since we've seen you.

RUDOLPH. Fourteen years.

CORNELIA. And you've fair filled out. Do you frequent a gymnasium?

VINCENT. I try to, I've a membership, good intentions.

CORNELIA. Matilda and me used to do Beverley Callard's *Rapid Results* once a quarter but the tape went and snapped, didn't it?

MATILDA. We had a similar body for a few months.

VINCENT. How's things with you, Rudolph?

CORNELIA. Poise yourself. And wait while I show you –

> CORNELIA *whips out an envelope, holds it out to* RUDOLPH.

> Take it.

> RUDOLPH *takes it*.

RUDOLPH. What is it?

CORNELIA (*to* VINCENT). A letter, come this morning for him and rightly so on such a joyous day of all days.

RUDOLPH. Come from where?

CORNELIA. I set to thinking you're wasting your time doing that Judy and Punch show to an empty seaside.

VINCENT. I didn't think you'd still do Judy and Punch.

RUDOLPH. It's not always empty.

CORNELIA. You can't very well expect a standing ovation from a dead swan and a Tampax. (*To* VINCENT.) Can he?

VINCENT. Rudolph?

RUDOLPH. I've always done it, Vincent. It's what I do.

CORNELIA. He's an ice-cream van he does it out the side of now, haven't you, Rudolph?

> RUDOLPH *opens the envelope, unfolds a letter, reads*.

RUDOLPH. The cardboard factory?

CORNELIA (*to* VINCENT). I'm sick to death of knitting him new crocodiles.

RUDOLPH. But I'm happy on that seaside –

CORNELIA (*to* VINCENT). I've only gone and scored him an interview.

RUDOLPH. I could add an extra show, do three Judy and Punches per day, seven days a week, every single day –

CORNELIA. They make Smarties tubes, Rudolph. You like Smarties.

RUDOLPH. Not since they went hexagonal.

CORNELIA. Do you know what Smarties are, Vincent?

VINCENT. Course.

CORNELIA. Well, they do the tubes for them.

MATILDA. They don't put the Smarties in.

CORNELIA (*to* VINCENT). You'll have to excuse Matilda, she's selective hyperglycaemic.

(*To* RUDOLPH.) When I rang they said you could start on a packer's wage, four quid an hour, and it'll be good for you, socially educational for you.

(*To* MATILDA.) Won't it be the making of him, Matilda, tell Vincent?

MATILDA. It's a lovely factory.

RUDOLPH. But I love to entertain. That crocodile's like a son to me –

CORNELIA. You heard this, Vincent?

RUDOLPH. But, Mam –

CORNELIA (*snaps*). What? Thank you?

Do you even appreciate that I'm the only one under this roof aggressively addressing what's best for you?

He's like this now, Vincent, forever showing off.

RUDOLPH. Do I have to?

CORNELIA. Yes, you do have to.

RUDOLPH. It says the interview's tomorrow.

CORNELIA. So?

RUDOLPH. What about my matinee?

CORNELIA. There isn't to be a matinee. Not any more.

RUDOLPH. Someone might eventually come.

CORNELIA. You're going. End of.

What's your plans now you're back, Vincent?

VINCENT. I'm just playing it by ear.

MATILDA. We'll miss you on telly.

CORNELIA. Hardly when we've got him living and breathing in the flesh.

MATILDA. We watch you every day –

CORNELIA (*to* VINCENT). She's star-struck, ignore her. (*To* MATILDA.) Do you not need the toilet, Matilda?

VINCENT. I'd like to see it.

CORNELIA. What?

VINCENT. Rudolph's van. If he doesn't mind.

CORNELIA. But you've barely sipped your cream soda.

VINCENT. I could do with some fresh air –

RUDOLPH. It's sea air.

CORNELIA. And them onion rings'll not eat themselves –

VINCENT. But –

CORNELIA (*snaps*). No.

Let's all just sit for a bit. I'll start you another jumper. A bigger, better jumper, you can all sit and watch.

Matilda, toilet –

VINCENT *stands*.

VINCENT. We'll only be half an hour.

CORNELIA. Come on now, let's stop this silliness. There's not even owt worth seeing, it's just Rudolph showing off. Again.

RUDOLPH. It was his idea –

CORNELIA (*snaps, to* RUDOLPH). Stop showing off.

Vincent?

VINCENT. I used to love those Judy and Punch shows. They'll take me right back. Him as the couple. Me as the crocodile.

RUDOLPH. They're still as good.

CORNELIA. It's not you that's forced to knit them.

VINCENT. Half an hour, Mam. For old time's sake?

Beat.

CORNELIA (*reluctantly*). Make sure it only is though. I'm off out myself later, plans I can't shift, and I'd hate not to properly see you on your first day home.

VINCENT. I'm not going anywhere.

CORNELIA. I do hope not.

(*To* RUDOLPH.) And don't take him through the town square. They burnt another witch at lunchtime.

MATILDA. We heard her screech from here.

CORNELIA. She thought someone had stepped on a hedgehog. Do you know what a hedgehog is, Vincent?

VINCENT. Course.

CORNELIA. I've never heard anything like it. So steer clear cos her charred skeleton'll still be up outside of what used to be Woolies.

MATILDA. Poor Mrs Pink.

VINCENT. What had she done?

CORNELIA. They never specifically said but folk wouldn't just go round setting other folk ablaze for nowt now, would they?

MATILDA. It was Whitney from Wilkinson's last week.

RUDOLPH. We all went along to watch.

CORNELIA. And what a lovely afternoon it was.

RUDOLPH. They hung her, Vincent.

CORNELIA. Do you wanna take a bag of Wotsits each? Or a Fondant Fancy, won't you take a Fancy?

VINCENT. Course.

CORNELIA. Course.

CORNELIA *hands* VINCENT *a French Fancy.*

There you go. Not completely useless, am I?

VINCENT. We'll not be long.

CORNELIA. Come here –

CORNELIA *hugs* VINCENT.

I bloody love you, you know.

VINCENT. And you.

CORNELIA. It's so lovely to see you. I know I've said it but it's true.

Why have you come home, love?

VINCENT. It's gonna be dark soon.

CORNELIA. You're right, get yourselves away and be boys, be brothers.

CORNELIA *pats* RUDOLPH *on the head.*

Look after him, you.

RUDOLPH. I will.

Exit VINCENT *and* RUDOLPH.

Across the next section, CORNELIA *applies a thick face of make-up.*

MATILDA *picks at the buffet.*

MATILDA. He's lovely, isn't he?

CORNELIA. They broke the mould with that one, love. Smashed it to smithereens and so elegantly more exotic than that lad of yours.

MATILDA. I can tell they're brothers.

CORNELIA. And that's exactly why I insisted they dash off and spend some quality time together. Reacquaint themselves with that brotherly bond and touch base.

I'd've joined them myself but I'm meeting Warren for that Spanish-themed Spanish night on up The Cherry Blossom Tree.

He can take or leave that kind of foreign muck but he knows the chap what runs it and he's agreed to do us bubbly egg and chips for the same price as a two-bit tapas.

Warren's like me with eggs. A fiend.

MATILDA. I'd love to meet him.

CORNELIA. And you will. And you'll swoon. He's like a fat Morrissey. And completely head over heels in love with me, that lad worships the ground I bloody walk on.

MATILDA. He sounds like perfection.

CORNELIA. Saying that, if he's a single fault, as many men have, it's that he could do with trimming his pubes. It's like trying to find a hamster in shredded paper.

Though you'll be no stranger to that, having to muck out that thing of our Lucy's.

MATILDA. We'll have to introduce Vincent to her when they come back.

CORNELIA. She'll more than likely freak the shit out of him, but he's very open-minded when it comes to the disabled is our Vincent.

It's probably part and parcel of working in the arts.

He once pushed a broad bean up his nose and was tone deaf for a fortnight.

MATILDA. Wow.

CORNELIA. Wow indeed, love.

Have you fed it today? Our Lucy?

MATILDA. I'll do her tea in a bit.

CORNELIA. She'll be happy with a brown Fondant Fancy, makes no odds to the likes of her. I popped in on her before and she was just sat there staring at Roisin.

MATILDA. She's blind.

CORNELIA. You know what I mean. Staring in her general direction. Whistling.

MATILDA. I heard her.

CORNELIA. Truth be told, she puts me in mind of a young Roger Whittaker.

MATILDA. She'd like that.

CORNELIA. Like what?

MATILDA. The comparison.

CORNELIA. And how on earth can you fathom what on earth that creature likes and dislikes?

MATILDA. I just think it's mother's intuition to know.

The lights snap to black.

Scene Two

Later that night.

MATILDA *is sat on the sofa holding a dildo.*

VINCENT *is opposite her with an Ann Summers handbook, he's testing her, animating a selection of sex toys to help her remember.*

They're both drinking wine.

MATILDA. It's got four speeds. Fingering, foreplay, fast and –

Furious?

VINCENT. Furious. Well done, you.

MATILDA. It's called a Rampant Rabbit Thruster –

Thruster –

Thruster –

I can't remember.

VINCENT. Rampant Rabbit Thruster Deluxe, you're almost there. Now what does it also come in?

MATILDA. Slim Wave. Platinum Plus. Aqua Adonis. Horny Heart-throb.

And Diamante?

VINCENT. And what do you need to warn the client re: the Diamante model?

MATILDA. What with it being that bit more bulky, the client'll consequently be sacrificing speed for visual bling.

VINCENT. Sold.

Don't look so worried. You've almost got it.

MATILDA. Cornelia said it would be like those Tupperware parties she did in the eighties.

VINCENT. I remember.

MATILDA. But it's just so much to remember.

VINCENT. You've got genuine potential, Matilda.

MATILDA *smiles, suddenly self-conscious.*

I had a lush walk back along the seafront.

MATILDA. All on your own?

VINCENT. It's never changed in all this time. Rudolph wanted some food.

MATILDA. Has something happened?

VINCENT. He went to that takeaway that used to be Barratts.

MATILDA. Curry Face?

VINCENT. That's the one.

Cheers.

They chink and drink.

We saw a tiger up the seafront.

MATILDA. When they closed down the zoo, they auctioned off the animals to the locals. He must've escaped. That tiger. We used to have a monkey. Rudolph said he'd always wanted a monkey as a living friend.

VINCENT. What kind of monkey?

MATILDA. Black and white. There's pictures of him somewhere with it on his shoulder.

VINCENT. Like Ross from *Friends*?

MATILDA. I don't really have any friends.

VINCENT. It's a programme.

MATILDA. Lucy's my best friend.

I can introduce you to Lucy in the morning, if you like?

VINCENT. Lucy?

MATILDA. Our daughter.

VINCENT. Rudolph never said.

MATILDA. She lives upstairs. She's deaf, dumb and blind.

Don't be sad. She's got a budgie called Roisin. Which is what I wanted to call her but Rudolph liked Lucy better. So I named the budgie. It was too exotic a name to waste, I thought.

Lucy copies her whistling. She whistles all day. Like a singing kettle.

VINCENT. How old is she?

MATILDA. Two at the weekend. She's beautiful.

But she's like that cos of what I did. It's my punishment, Cornelia says. They both say. But I didn't do anything wrong, Vincent. Not really.

VINCENT. These things just happen.

MATILDA. They happen to me all the time.

What happened to you? Why have you come home?

VINCENT. Does there have to be a reason?

MATILDA. To come here? Yes.

VINCENT. I just fancied it.

MATILDA. You look fatter on the telly.

VINCENT. Thanks.

MATILDA. Do you write the stories yourself?

VINCENT. We tend to use existing ones. Fairytales and picture books.

MATILDA. I'm writing a book, Vincent.

VINCENT. What kind of book?

MATILDA. A novel.

VINCENT. Has it got a title?

MATILDA. *Shine*.

Do you want to hear a bit?

VINCENT. I'd love to.

MATILDA *stands, eyes closed, recites from memory:*

MATILDA. *Shine* by Matilda Glass.

Laura escapes it all. The hurly-burly grey of life. Her lonely little existence. For one unforgettable summer in Malia.

Because all Laura has ever wanted is to feel the sea tickling her toes. A fine wine coursing through her veins. The shine of the sun blinding her tired eyes.

But in the island's speedboat enthusiast Christian, Laura finds a kindred spirit. And what begins as the search for happiness, leads to something more blinding than the sun.

It leads Laura to a perfect kind of love.

The kind of love people sing songs about.

MATILDA *opens her eyes*.

That was it. That was *Shine*.

VINCENT. It's really powerful.

MATILDA. I saw a documentary on Malia. And there was sun everywhere.

Cos Laura has sex in it with a man on a speedboat. A man a million miles away from any man she's ever seen.

And no one's even driving that speedboat, Vincent. It's just zooming out to sea with Laura and Christian on the back of it. Going at it. Over and over and over, Vincent. Determined sex –

MATILDA *realises she's still holding the dildo, pops it on the floor.*

Laura's free, you see.

VINCENT. I like the sound of Christian.

MATILDA. I like talking to you. And I'm glad you've come back to us. Whatever your real reason is.

VINCENT. I've told you what it is.

MATILDA. Course you have.

VINCENT *tops up their drinks.*

VINCENT. I didn't recognise a single soul up The Cherry Blossom Tree.

MATILDA. Was it packed?

VINCENT. Heaving.

MATILDA. But it was nice?

VINCENT. I met someone.

MATILDA. Who?

VINCENT. Edward. He works up the baker's. He's the baker's son.

MATILDA. I think I know who you mean.

VINCENT. He's lovely, isn't he? He's beautiful.

MATILDA. I suppose so.

VINCENT. You know I'm gay, don't you, Matilda?

MATILDA. You look gay.

VINCENT. He's not like anyone I know in that city.

Enter RUDOLPH, *he's pissed*.

RUDOLPH. Where did you go?

VINCENT. I said I was coming back.

RUDOLPH. I got chips.

VINCENT. Where are they?

RUDOLPH. I eat them in your absence.

VINCENT. That's alright.

RUDOLPH. I know it's alright.

VINCENT. Me and Matilda were just getting to know each other a bit better.

RUDOLPH. You missed some lad getting battered outside Curry Face, an Asian lad, five foot high if he was a day.

MATILDA. Is he okay?

RUDOLPH. The JD Sports lads kicked the living shite out of him. There was loads of us watching in a circle. It was mint.

VINCENT. Would you like a glass of wine?

RUDOLPH (*mocking*). 'Would you like a glass of wine'?

VINCENT. That's what I said.

RUDOLPH. I've some vodka upstairs, if you'd rather?

MATILDA. Where've you got vodka?

RUDOLPH (*to* VINCENT). I stash it in Lucy's room.

MATILDA. Will you pop some trill out for Roisin while you're there?

RUDOLPH (*mocking*). 'Pop some trill out for Roisin while you're there' –

Exit RUDOLPH.

MATILDA. He's drunk.

VINCENT. It's fine.

You won't say anything, will you? About Edward.

MATILDA. No.

VINCENT. No. Lush. Thank you.

Is Mam out with Auntie Crystal?

MATILDA. Warren. He's her fancy man. It's a love job.

VINCENT. What's he like?

MATILDA. I've not met him. But he sounds dead romantic.

VINCENT. What's Mam said?

MATILDA. He's got long pubes, Vincent.

Enter RUDOLPH, *brandishing half a bottle of cheap vodka.*

RUDOLPH. She's whistling her tits off up there. Have you even fed her?

MATILDA. She's had three brown French Fancies.

RUDOLPH. As long as it was just the brown.

(*To* MATILDA.) Have you been drinking?

MATILDA. I've got a white wine.

RUDOLPH (*mocking*). 'I've got a white wine.'

MATILDA. Stop it.

RUDOLPH (*to* VINCENT). She never normally drinks, it sends her wacky. She had a sip of Mam's Baileys at Christmas and was under that table for an hour convinced she was a prisoner of war.

(*To* MATILDA.) We had to tease you out in the end with a Big Purple Quality Street, didn't we?

MATILDA (*to* VINCENT). I wasn't well, I'd had the runs all that week.

RUDOLPH. I'd pay good money to see you on spirits.

MATILDA. I don't mind trying some.

RUDOLPH. Tough shite.

VINCENT. I'll have one, if you're offering?

RUDOLPH. The Milky Bars are on me, Vincent.

Over the next section, RUDOLPH *prepares two beakers of vodka and cream soda, hands one to* VINCENT.

We raped that gambler in The Cherry Blossom, didn't we?

VINCENT. We did.

RUDOLPH. Twenty chunks, Matilda. I says, I may very well be on the bones of my own arse but I still stretched to some Aftershocks.

VINCENT. He did.

RUDOLPH. Him on a CBBC wage, me on my last ounce of baccy and still it was me splashing the cash, me treating my own flesh and my own blood. Ten Aftershocks, Matilda, not one.

MATILDA. I'm allergic to Aftershock.

RUDOLPH. You've never even had it. (*To* VINCENT.) Rocket fuel to the likes of her. (*To* MATILDA.) We should give our Lucy one one time just to see what she does –

MATILDA. Stop showing off –

RUDOLPH (*snaps*). I'm not showing off.

I'm always like this. She'd maybes get a taste for it and we'd not be able to shut the bitch up.

Be a welcome relief from having to listen to you twenty-four fucking seven.

MATILDA. She's dumb.

RUDOLPH. You are.

MATILDA. I wonder what she'd say if she had a voice.

RUDOLPH. Ignore her, she's pissed.

RUDOLPH *plonks himself down on the sofa.*

What did you want with that lad in The Cherry Blossom?

VINCENT. I can't even remember his name –

RUDOLPH. Edward.

VINCENT. It's them Aftershocks, I can barely remember my own.

MATILDA. Will you see him again?

RUDOLPH. He'll not have time in just a few days.

Will you, Vincent?

VINCENT. I could always stay a while longer.

RUDOLPH. Why when there's nothing here for you?

MATILDA. He doesn't have to go. (*To* VINCENT.) It's Lucy's party at the weekend –

RUDOLPH. But if he's plans –

MATILDA. I know she'd love to have her favourite uncle there –

RUDOLPH. If he's said, Matilda. If he's already promised –

VINCENT. We'll see, won't we.

MATILDA. There must be loads you've missed after so long.

VINCENT. Course. Cos some of it's not changed a stitch. But then there's other things I can't even ever remember being here –

RUDOLPH. What did you miss most?

VINCENT. The sea. That ten-a-penny rock shop. Lorraine's lighthouse.

It's funny what you forget after so long –

RUDOLPH. It's where you're from. Whether you like it or not.

VINCENT. Course.

RUDOLPH. How do you know him, then? This Edward.

VINCENT. I've said. I don't really.

Enter CORNELIA, *she's pissed.*

CORNELIA. Here's my boy, my pride and my beautiful joy, come here, love –

CORNELIA *drunkenly hugs* VINCENT, *pats* RUDOLPH'*s head*.

MATILDA. Did you have fun?

CORNELIA. I. Am. Fucked.

MATILDA. How was Warren?

CORNELIA. I reckon it was that bubbly egg. I says, here, San Diego del Whatever-the-fuck-your-name-is, the chap what runs the tapas, I says, your eggs are off. He says, 'Fuck off.' I says, no, you fuck off.

You couldn't fault his chips, mind, Vincent, they were crisp, they were dry and I had this lovely little cocktail that was to die for, not too offensive just fruity and juicy like a little fruit juice.

I says, I'll be back here for another one of them but you can keep your eggs. I never want to see another egg as long as I live, even a Creme Egg and you know how I love Creme Eggs.

Tell Vincent how much I love Creme Eggs, Matilda.

MATILDA. She has three a week.

CORNELIA. Four a week. Sometimes five.

Where'd you pair get to?

VINCENT. Just for a swift half after I'd seen his van –

RUDOLPH. We've had ten Aftershocks.

CORNELIA. We all should've met up. We'll have to do that one time.

MATILDA. That'd be lovely.

CORNELIA. I can't recall anyone ever inviting you.

CORNELIA *slumps onto* VINCENT'*s knee, clings to him*.

Oh, how I have missed you. What's this you're drinking?

RUDOLPH. Cream soda.

CORNELIA. I was actually asking my son, Rudolph.

VINCENT. Cream soda.

CORNELIA. Let's all have a party, it's only early. (*To* RUDOLPH.) Get the record player on. (*To* MATILDA.) You, go and get Lucy.

MATILDA. She's asleep.

CORNELIA. Then wake her –

(*To* VINCENT.) She plays this game, Vincent. You ask her a question and tell her one whistle for 'yes' and two for 'no', you ask her any question, any one in this whole wide world and Lucy'll tell you the answer.

I dunno how, she's deaf, midwife said.

She's psychic, though, isn't she, Matilda? She's haunted. Go and get her, bring her to her favourite nana –

MATILDA. No.

CORNELIA. Pissed, I'm assuming, are you? Snappy.

MATILDA. Sorry.

CORNELIA. Wait while I show you all this –

CORNELIA *pulls a shirt from her handbag, hands it to* RUDOLPH.

I got it from Warren for your interview tomorrow, isn't it lush? (*To* MATILDA.) You. Pass my knitting. I need calming down after the way you've just spoken to me.

MATILDA *passes* CORNELIA *her knitting, she knits as:*

(*To* RUDOLPH.) Well, don't just sit there gawping at it, get it on.

RUDOLPH *holds up the shirt. It's massive.*

RUDOLPH. It's huge.

CORNELIA. He didn't have to offer you it. (*To* MATILDA.) Needed more than his arm twisting, if you know what I mean?

RUDOLPH *reluctantly undresses, slips into the shirt.*

RUDOLPH. I don't like it.

CORNELIA. I think it's sexy, much less sexy than on my
    Warren but isn't it sexy, Vincent?

VINCENT. It's nice.

CORNELIA. Gorgeous. Isn't it, Matilda?

MATILDA. It's a bit big.

CORNELIA. Do you wanna take just five minutes off
    persecuting me?

MATILDA. How was Warren?

CORNELIA. Fit. As. Fuck.

RUDOLPH (*to* VINCENT). Can I not just borrow one of yours?

CORNELIA. Had his floppy hair swept to one side when I
    walked in and did this hilarious trick where he blew it up
    with a straw. I actually physically pissed myself.

VINCENT (*to* RUDOLPH). I don't really have any dressy shirts.

CORNELIA. He's fine with that one.

VINCENT. We could nip into town early tomorrow, if you like?
    I'll treat you to one from Matalan.

RUDOLPH. I'd love that –

CORNELIA. No. I won't have you wasting good money,
    Vincent, not on him, he'll not get the wear. (*To* RUDOLPH.)
    You'll not get the wear, Rudolph –

VINCENT. I don't mind.

RUDOLPH. I will get the wear.

CORNELIA. Tuck it in, if you tuck it in it'll not look so
    enormous on you – (*To* MATILDA.) here –

    CORNELIA *hands her knitting to* MATILDA, *tucks*
    RUDOLPH's *shirt in, smartens him up like a schoolboy.*

    Making out you're skin and bone, you're far from it, an
    extra-extra-large if you're a day –

RUDOLPH. I can do it myself –

CORNELIA. Evidently not.

Look at the plight of him, everyone. What a silly, sorry state of a sexless man –

CORNELIA *takes a hankerchief from her pocket, gobs on it, wipes around* RUDOLPH*'s mouth.*

RUDOLPH. Mam –

CORNELIA. There you are. Cute as a button. If you don't get that job tomorrow it'll not be this shirt's fault. (*To* MATILDA.) Tell him.

MATILDA. It won't be that shirt's fault.

CORNELIA. Come and I'll show you where you'll be sleeping, Vincent.

CORNELIA *grabs* VINCENT*'s hand, pulls him up to stand.*

We'll pop you in the honeymoon suite, first floor, sea view.

VINCENT. I know where it is.

CORNELIA. It's our finest room. Princess Diana's words, not mine.

MATILDA. When was the people's princess here?

CORNELIA. We struggled to keep her away, back when this was the only guesthouse for miles and the sea was all fields.

She doted on our Vincent.

MATILDA. Wow.

CORNELIA. Wow indeed, love.

(*To* VINCENT.) You'll have to excuse the ghost of your great-great-grandmother Gloria von Glass but she's more a banger than a scratcher these days.

But, for a woman forced to give birth on that landing, biting down on nothing more than a bit of flapjack, I think she's earned the odd rat-a-tat-tat, don't you?

And everyone needs someone to watch over them.

I hear her haunting that first-floor corridor and dread the day she finds a stained bed sheet or, God forbid, the odd stray pube. I'll be forced to shear Warren like a sheep.

She always was a very anally-retentive matriarch.

VINCENT. That's comforting to know.

CORNELIA. Come on, special son –

CORNELIA *drags* VINCENT *to the door*.

VINCENT. Night, you two.

RUDOLPH. Night.

CORNELIA *and* VINCENT *exit*.

MATILDA. Sweet dreams, Vincent.

RUDOLPH *goes to the door, stands in front of it, desperate to follow.*

MATILDA *goes over to him.*

Did you have a good night?

RUDOLPH *punches* MATILDA *in the stomach, she doubles over, drops to the floor.*

RUDOLPH. Posh fucker.

Lighting change.

Enter VINCENT. *He unfolds the sofa to pull out a children's TV-style craft table complete with sticky-back plastic dispenser, pipe cleaners, school glue.*

Over the next section, he fashions a papier mâché crocodile as if to a nation of craft crazy kids.

VINCENT. Once upon a time there was a lonely crocodile that lived in the sea by a seaside town.

He didn't have a name because no one had ever given him one. And he didn't have any friends because a lonely crocodile is the hungriest of all crocodiles.

'Will you be my friend?' he could be heard screaming from the safe cobbled streets of the seaside town. But no one ever came. No one dared.

Because everybody knew that if they stepped so much as one footstep into that sea, the lonely crocodile with his empty stomach would snap them up between his angry jaws.

The lights snap to black.

Scene Three

The next morning.

RUDOLPH *is pressed and dressed, downstage centre in a chair, cloaked in towels with a manic* CORNELIA *behind him, hacking in an interview hairdo.*

VINCENT *is at the table, engrossed in the local newspaper.*

CORNELIA. Sit up straight or you'll come out wonky.

RUDOLPH *straightens up.*

Better.

It'll do you the world of good, this. Get you out that ice-cream van for good. And I'm not saying you've much to offer but those ten hours a day'll be better served up that factory than in that van.

I remember a time you used to hate it, a time I used to have to lock you in and leave you. Terrified of being alone. Not like my Vincent. (*To* VINCENT.) Isn't that right, love?

VINCENT. What?

CORNELIA. You. A loner in the very best sense of the word. Popular. Intelligent. Independent.

VINCENT. I dunno about that.

CORNELIA. He claims to love it now but I remember a time he craved nothing but company.

(*To* RUDOLPH.) Is that lock still there I bolted to the outside of the door?

RUDOLPH. Yeah.

CORNELIA. Sign of quality that. And you grew to love it eventually. Waiting all hours until I'd come and free you.

I pissed myself that time you'd shit yourself.

CORNELIA *catches* RUDOLPH*'s ear with the scissors.*

RUDOLPH. Ow –

CORNELIA *belts* RUDOLPH *round the head.*

CORNELIA. I won't tell you again.

RUDOLPH. Sorry.

CORNELIA *continues to cut.*

CORNELIA (*to* VINCENT). Is there anything in there about that lad what used to work the funfair with your Uncle Jacob?

VINCENT. Where?

CORNELIA. Your paper.

VINCENT. I don't think so.

CORNELIA. Guillotined himself, didn't he, Rudolph?

RUDOLPH. He did.

CORNELIA. Sit straight.

Fashioned a home-made contraption from bits of the upside-down rocket ride, set a timer up and –

VINCENT. And what?

CORNELIA. Anaesthetised himself with fourteen blisters of paracetamol and a blue WKD. Settled down to sleep under it and was found the next day. His head rolled off.

He was only seventeen.

VINCENT. Why would he do that?

CORNELIA. Some say he'd been with a black lass, others he was gay, either way, he's better off dead.

(*To* RUDOLPH.) I've often wondered what you'd look like without a head –

RUDOLPH *flinches*.

(*Snaps*.) Still, I said.

And don't dare tell them you can't read.

VINCENT. He can read.

CORNELIA. Well, he can't write and, traditionally, the two come hand in hand. (*To* RUDOLPH.) About turn –

CORNELIA *takes a tub of wet-look hair gel, chuckles to herself.*

RUDOLPH. What?

CORNELIA. Sometimes you look so bloody comical.

(*To* VINCENT.) Doesn't he look like a koala?

VINCENT. He looks fine.

CORNELIA. He looks stupid.

VINCENT. And he'll look even better once we smarten him up.

CORNELIA. I suppose of anyone you'd know best.

VINCENT. Why don't you go and dig out one of Dad's old ties?

CORNELIA (*to* RUDOLPH). See? I pray for the day you're as forward-thinking as your baby brother.

VINCENT. There must be one somewhere.

CORNELIA. I do distinctly remember seeing a Homer Simpson one. You never know, it might inject you with a modicum of personality.

CORNELIA *hands the hair gel to* VINCENT *and exits.*

RUDOLPH. Thank you.

VINCENT. Do you want me to try and tidy you up a bit?

RUDOLPH. Do I look shite?

VINCENT. Not completely.

RUDOLPH. Please.

Over the next section, VINCENT *styles* RUDOLPH*'s hair with gel.*

You know that lad she said about?

VINCENT. The one without a head?

RUDOLPH. He was Warren's son.

VINCENT. Does Mam know?

RUDOLPH. Everyone knows. Cos Warren's bad news. Too bad even to be in that paper.

VINCENT. Hold still.

Are you nervous?

RUDOLPH. How do you know Edward?

VINCENT. Friend of a friend.

RUDOLPH. I didn't think you had any here.

VINCENT. They're not important.

RUDOLPH. Then neither is Edward. Is he?

VINCENT. You've funny hair.

RUDOLPH. Koala hair?

VINCENT. Felt hair. My ex was a hairdresser, used to say my hair was like felt. Nowt much you can ever do with it.

RUDOLPH. What was she like?

VINCENT. Who?

RUDOLPH. Your ex?

VINCENT. Lush.

RUDOLPH. What were her tits like?

VINCENT. It was a long time ago.

RUDOLPH. Like melons, I imagine. A lad like you. Looking like you.

Matilda's are shite tits.

VINCENT. Hold still.

RUDOLPH. Mam's are massive, like sporrans.

She loves having you here. She's different when you're here. Different with you than me.

VINCENT. It's just the novelty. That'll soon wear off.

RUDOLPH. Do you feel you've come home? Like properly in your heart of heart's home?

VINCENT. I suppose.

RUDOLPH. Is it wonderful where you are?

VINCENT. Remember when you were little and your hair forever stuck up at the front?

RUDOLPH. I would love to know what you're like there.

VINCENT. Try as she might, no amount of Mam's spit could weigh it down.

RUDOLPH. How different you are there.

VINCENT. What you see is what you get.

RUDOLPH. How delightful you are.

VINCENT. It's not that different to here you know, Rudolph.

RUDOLPH. But are you that different? Cos there's folk say it's like living in Christmas. That all that excitement changes you.

VINCENT. I'm still the same, aren't I?

RUDOLPH. You're not. You're exotic now, Vincent.

VINCENT. All done.

RUDOLPH. Thank you.

VINCENT *moves around to face* RUDOLPH, *pulls him up in front of him, a few finishing touches to his fringe.*

VINCENT. You'll get that job, you know. You deserve that job. You've earned it.

RUDOLPH. Really?

VINCENT. You look cool, Rudolph. You should make an effort more.

RUDOLPH. You think I look lovely?

VINCENT. You do –

> RUDOLPH *kisses* VINCENT *on the lips*. VINCENT *pulls back*.

> RUDOLPH *ruffles up his hair, feels it*.

RUDOLPH. It feels dead different.

VINCENT. I should go.

RUDOLPH. Where?

VINCENT. I'm meeting Edward.

RUDOLPH. But you didn't even remember his name.

VINCENT. I was drunk.

RUDOLPH. Not important, you said.

VINCENT. He asked. I should've said no.

RUDOLPH. I could come?

VINCENT. You've your interview.

RUDOLPH. I'll never get it. I can't even count.

VINCENT. Everyone can count.

RUDOLPH. I don't want it.

VINCENT. Have you practised your answers? Cos they'll ask why you want this job in particular.

RUDOLPH. I want to come with you.

VINCENT. Don't say you've the ability to work well as an individual but also as part of a team. Everyone says that, they expect that.

RUDOLPH. I want it to be like when we were little. When we'd run along to the funfair like we were dashing to the end of the earth for its fun.

VINCENT. Don't let them see you coming.

RUDOLPH. When you promised we could leave together.

VINCENT. We're all grown up now.

RUDOLPH. Why have you really come home after all this time?

VINCENT. It's a holiday. People take holidays, Rudolph.

RUDOLPH. They never come here. So there has to be something else.

Something has to have gone wrong.

VINCENT. Can we do this later?

RUDOLPH. Tonight?

VINCENT. I don't know.

RUDOLPH. Matilda's got her Ann Summers party upstairs. She's put a card in the newsagent's.

VINCENT. I'm gonna be late.

RUDOLPH. It's gonna be bedlam. I'll make tea. I'll expect you.

Cos I might look like I've got it all. But it's your company I crave.

MATILDA *appears in the hall door with a garish Homer Simpson tie.*

MATILDA. Your mam said to give you this.

RUDOLPH. I'm not wearing it.

VINCENT. He's just nervous. Come on, Rudolph. It's cool.

RUDOLPH. I've never put one on before. Have you?

VINCENT. I've got to go. Matilda's here. Good luck.

MATILDA. Bye, Vincent.

RUDOLPH. We did it all the time when we were little, Vincent.

I'll expect you.

Exit VINCENT.

MATILDA. I can do it. Here.

Over the next section, MATILDA *loops the tie round* RUDOLPH*'s neck, ties it.*

I was thinking we could get Lucy some new clothes with the money from your job. They grow so fast at her age.

RUDOLPH. I wouldn't know.

MATILDA. Two at the weekend. She's so excited. I think she knows what's coming.

RUDOLPH. Maybe you could get yourself some while you're at it?

MATILDA. I'll be making an effort this evening. The Ann Summers rep should ooze sex. The handbook says.

RUDOLPH. You can't polish a turd, Matilda.

MATILDA *finishes* RUDOLPH*'s tie, straightens it.*

MATILDA. I've just finished a really interesting passage of my novel. Would you like to have a look before you go?

RUDOLPH. I'm alright.

MATILDA. It's about the first time Laura meets Christian. It's starlight under a gazebo and she's feeling glamorous for the first time ever.

He gives her a red rose. No talking. No nothing. Just a single red rose.

A language that's just theirs. The language of love.

RUDOLPH. I don't speak Spanish.

MATILDA. It's in English, silly.

RUDOLPH. I don't care if it's in Braille on Cindy Crawford's tits.

MATILDA. Do you want me to walk along with you?

RUDOLPH. I can manage.

MATILDA. I can tell you're nervous. But please don't be.

RUDOLPH. I'm already missing Judy and Punch.

MATILDA. Why don't you take them with you?

RUDOLPH. They're already in my pocket.

MATILDA. You're a wonderful man, Rudolph Glass.

RUDOLPH. Am I?

MATILDA. Everyone says. And look at you. I'm as proud as that punch.

RUDOLPH. I feel stupid, Matilda.

MATILDA. Kiss for luck?

RUDOLPH *takes a red balloon from his pocket, begins to blow it up.*

Your mam's upstairs.

RUDOLPH *continues until the balloon is at maximum capacity, ties it, hands it to* MATILDA, *she takes it with both hands.*

RUDOLPH. If you close your eyes it'll hurt less.

MATILDA *closes her eyes as* RUDOLPH *kisses her, they have sex on the sofa as:*

Lighting change.

Enter VINCENT. *He unfolds the sofa to pull out his craft table.*

Over the next section, he finishes his papier mâché crocodile.

VINCENT. As the years passed, the people of the town stopped hearing the screams of the lonely crocodile. But, more importantly, they forgot to keep telling his story.

And so when one little boy followed the sun down to the seaside, he thought nothing of slipping off his socks and shoes, of paddling out until the sea was up to his knees.

One little boy that was never seen again. Because lonely, hungry crocodiles love little boys.

And so his story started again, along the safe cobbled streets of the same seaside town. As mothers warned their children and doctors warned their patients, never to go into the sea because the crocodile will get you.

A crocodile so lonely, so sad, and with such an empty echoing stomach, that he'll gobble you up whole.

The lights snap to black.

Scene Four

Later that day.

The dining table is downstage centre, RUDOLPH *at one end,*
VINCENT *at the other, wearing matching jumpers, each with
their name knitted into the front in a garish colourful font.*

*They're eating spaghetti and hot-dog sausages, there's a candle
and wine.*

RUDOLPH. They're ringing in a couple of days. Three tops.

VINCENT. That's promising. That's swift.

RUDOLPH. They did an informative introduction about making
cardboard. Its journey from thick porridge-like substance,
through pressing and printing, to nationwide distribution.

Which means some of it probably ends up somewhere near
you.

VINCENT. It certainly sounds like it's gone in.

RUDOLPH. They thought I was shite.

VINCENT. Did they say that?

RUDOLPH *eats.*

Did you get any free Smarties?

RUDOLPH. There was a plate of Custard Creams on the table.
They manufacture the corrugated card that slips inside the
pack to keep them from crumbling. It was a free sample.

VINCENT. Lucky lot.

RUDOLPH. I didn't take one.

VINCENT. I'd've applied myself for a free Fox's Crunch
Cream.

RUDOLPH. Are they a city delicacy?

VINCENT. They're ten-a-penny.

RUDOLPH. Ten of your pennies, not mine.

VINCENT. I'll take you up the Spar tomorrow, buy you a pack.

RUDOLPH *holds his fork midair, above his lap, freezes, as:*

RUDOLPH. You'd do that for me?

VINCENT *nods.*

A sausage falls from RUDOLPH*'s fork, drops to his trousers.*

Shite –

VINCENT *hands* RUDOLPH *his napkin, drapes it across* RUDOLPH*'s knee.*

VINCENT. You put this over your knee to avoid spillages.

RUDOLPH. I didn't know.

They eat.

VINCENT. I saw Edward this afternoon.

RUDOLPH. You've said.

VINCENT. He showed me his cakes.

RUDOLPH. You can't've had anything to talk about.

VINCENT. They were almost too beautiful to eat –

RUDOLPH. So they could've been nicer?

VINCENT. He had one he was trialling for a wedding. Some young lass from along the shore –

RUDOLPH. Spanner Karen. She courts Lionel from the swimming baths.

VINCENT. She'd given him a drawing of what she wanted.

RUDOLPH. What did you talk about?

VINCENT. Just crayon and a splash of glitter pen. And I don't know how but he'd managed it. Line for line. Smudge for sparkly smudge.

RUDOLPH. He'll've seen you on the telly and want you to make him famous.

VINCENT. He'd realised the whole thing in piping and icing.

RUDOLPH. Do you miss being on the telly?

VINCENT. I was just saying.

RUDOLPH. Do you?

VINCENT. It's just a job at the end of the day.

RUDOLPH. So you're not going back? You've definitely been sacked?

VINCENT. It's not as glamorous as it looks, Rudolph.

RUDOLPH. But you have left? Walked out? All guns a-blazing?

VINCENT. I've taken unpaid leave.

RUDOLPH. 'A holiday', you said.

VINCENT. It's the same thing.

RUDOLPH. Indefinitely?

VINCENT. Eat up. Pasta's shit at holding its heat.

VINCENT eats.

RUDOLPH. When are you leaving?

VINCENT. Do you not want me here?

RUDOLPH. It's a simple question.

VINCENT. I never knew you could cook. This is nice.

They eat.

RUDOLPH. You're lucky. I'd love a holiday.

VINCENT. You should take one.

RUDOLPH. I could've done.

VINCENT. You and Matilda.

RUDOLPH. You and me.

VINCENT. For fuck's sake, Rudolph –

RUDOLPH. Together we always said.

VINCENT. I was sixteen.

RUDOLPH. You promised.

VINCENT. We were bits of kids.

RUDOLPH. You never even said goodbye.

VINCENT. I'm back now, aren't I? I'm here now.

RUDOLPH. You've not even apologised.

VINCENT. You could still go.

RUDOLPH. With you?

VINCENT. With anyone. Nothing's ever stopped you.

RUDOLPH. There's crocodiles in the water, Vincent.

VINCENT. Is there?

RUDOLPH. They're everywhere, Mam said. And crocodiles love boys.

VINCENT. I won't apologise.

RUDOLPH. I wouldn't accept it even if you did.

They eat.

VINCENT. You've your whole life here. You've a family.

RUDOLPH. That never stopped you.

VINCENT. This is where you belong. The grass is never ever greener.

RUDOLPH. It always is. And you know it.

VINCENT. Have you taken Lucy in the sea?

RUDOLPH. Are you deaf? It's too dangerous.

VINCENT. You could just paddle. Feed the senses she has got.

Push her along the prom in the sun, sit her in a dodgem, buy her some candyfloss. Can you imagine being able to have candyfloss for the first time again?

I don't know –

RUDOLPH. No, you don't.

VINCENT. I met her earlier. She's very special.

RUDOLPH. Special needs?

VINCENT. She's extraordinary. That smile.

RUDOLPH. That bird. That budgie.

VINCENT. Roisin.

RUDOLPH. I love that little feathered thing. Sneak up every night when everyone's asleep and stroke her in the dark. I teach her to whistle such wonderful tunes, Vincent.

Tunes that she teaches Lucy. Ones I never could. Ones I can't.

Cos I can touch that bird. Its fluttering feathers, claws, beak, shite. But her skin. Lucy's skin. It makes my fucking skin crawl.

VINCENT. But you're her dad.

RUDOLPH. You're right. Pasta's shite at holding its heat.

They eat.

VINCENT. It's nice to see you've cracked spaghetti.

RUDOLPH. Sorry?

VINCENT. Remember there was a time you couldn't work it?

RUDOLPH. I was fine with hoops.

VINCENT. They don't count.

RUDOLPH. They don't really, do they?

You don't have to stay in that haunted room, if you don't want? There's always an empty bunk below me.

VINCENT. I don't mind.

RUDOLPH. Do you remember that bunk? Making it into all manner of camps and dens. Hiding in there from Mam on bath night. Bubble-bath hair and beards. Kissing in the cupboard.

Do you remember, Vincent?

VINCENT. Is there wine in this?

RUDOLPH. Shite-loads.

VINCENT. I can tell. Of course I remember.

RUDOLPH. Warren taught Mam and she taught me. About wine in food.

VINCENT. He certainly sounds like he knows his stuff.

RUDOLPH *pushes his plate to one side, wipes his mouth with his napkin, necks his wine.*

RUDOLPH. Warren raped someone. He's a rapist. Mam knows but she's pretending it's not happening.

VINCENT. And is it?

RUDOLPH. What?

VINCENT. Happening.

RUDOLPH. Why would someone make something like that up?

VINCENT. I don't know.

RUDOLPH. Everyone says.

VINCENT. I've decided to stay until Lucy's party and then I'm going.

RUDOLPH. She won't even know you're here.

VINCENT. She will. And then I'm gone.

RUDOLPH. You're staying for Edward.

VINCENT *eats.*

I sit in that ice-cream van looking out to sea. And not just checking for crocodiles. I bought some binoculars.

And I stare across to see if I can see it. Your city. You in it. You doing whatever you like to do in it. Whatever you can cos you're there and not here.

I sometimes see lights, Vincent. And, if I listen hard enough, hear people. People living lives that people can live there. Lives we all should be able to live.

Even someone like me.

VINCENT. You haven't got a clue.

RUDOLPH. I have. And it's stupid. But in my head that's what your city is. It's not having to worry. It's feeling real.

VINCENT. You are stupid. She's made you stupid.

RUDOLPH. Why did you come home, Vincent?

VINCENT *pours them both some wine, finishes his pasta, as:*

There was a woman came here looking for a room. Months back now.

We turned her away, had closed for business by then and sent her up The Tudor Rose. They've still two singles they let out from time to time, attic rooms, bitter cold, but 'try there', Mam said and off she went.

She crossed the town centre and happened upon the roofing lads rolling out The Cherry Blossom. They'd just won the cockfight in the cellar, rolling pissed and introduced themselves one by one. She checked she was heading in the right direction, asked them nice, polite, flashing her p's and her q's, not from round here, not normal.

So, they took her back into the pub. Said they'd show her some local hospitality, walk along to The Tudor themselves with her once they'd given her a proper seaside welcome.

I got all this from Gaz the labourer.

She said a bit about herself, like flies round shite they were, intrigued by her from the off. Until one tale led to another and she confused herself, corrected herself.

And they started to realise, they worked out from her story that she was that woman that protected that paedophile that killed those two girls down south.

The angel ones all smiles in football shirts.

'We don't want folk like you round here,' they'd said.

So they took her down to the cellar where they fight their cocks, their pitbulls, each other. It's so deep down in this ground, Vincent, that no one can hear you scream. She never made it to The Tudor Rose. They tore her limb from limb by all accounts.

Scattered her remains from the shoreline to the factory two days later as a warning.

The police came over from the city. But they never found her face. It was her, though, Gaz said. That bitch from the front of the papers. It was obvious, he said. Hate hiding in her eyes.

We might not have motorways or McDonald's, Vincent. But we're not stupid. I'm not stupid.

VINCENT. I haven't done anything wrong.

Enter MATILDA, *in slutty finery.*

MATILDA. No one's come to my Ann Summers party.

RUDOLPH. Upstairs.

MATILDA. Has anyone knocked?

RUDOLPH. No.

MATILDA. Are you alright, Vincent? You've seen Gloria, haven't you?

VINCENT. I'm fine. Fine.

RUDOLPH. See? He's double fine. We'll see you in the morning. Get gone.

MATILDA. Come up for a bit if you like?

RUDOLPH. We're talking. Lad talk.

MATILDA. Well, just give me a shout if anyone comes. It's weird up there, just me and Lucy in our suspenders.

RUDOLPH. It's all for a good cause, now fuck off.

MATILDA. I will. Have a nice night, boys.

Exit MATILDA.

RUDOLPH *comes up behind* VINCENT, *massages his shoulders.*

RUDOLPH. Should we nip up The Cherry Blossom for last orders?

VINCENT. What happened to her face, Rudolph?

RUDOLPH. Gaz sold it to the butcher.

The lights snap to black.

Scene Five

The next day.

RUDOLPH *and* VINCENT *are sat on the carpet playing Guess Who?*

CORNELIA *is flapping about in the kitchen, heating up a light lunch.*

MATILDA *is on the sofa, rolling a pile of tangled wool around her fist, into fresh new balls.*

RUDOLPH. I've asked about Edward, you know.

VINCENT. Has yours got white hair?

RUDOLPH. They've not.

VINCENT. Like you asked about Warren?

    VINCENT *clacks some faces down.*

RUDOLPH. He's trouble. Everyone says.

VINCENT. Course he is.

RUDOLPH. Has yours got a hat?

VINCENT. And what do they say, Rudolph?

RUDOLPH. Well, has it?

VINCENT. No.

    That we're in love. That we've both already said it and meant it?

    That all we do is fuck? And then talk? And then fuck again? Over and over in filthy glory. In understanding. In tenderness.

    Is that what this town says?

    RUDOLPH *clacks some faces down.*

RUDOLPH. They say he's a nasty piece of work. That he once took a lass up Lily Piccadilly's, her that does abortions with an ear-piercing gun for a fiver and left her there to be butchered.

VINCENT. Is it ginger?

RUDOLPH. No.

VINCENT. What are you lying for?

VINCENT *clacks some faces down.*

RUDOLPH. Ask anyone, ask Lily Piccadilly –

VINCENT (*snaps*). I'm asking you –

CORNELIA (*off*). Red or brown sauce?

VINCENT. Red, please –

RUDOLPH. Brown. (*To* VINCENT.) Has yours got a beard?

CORNELIA (*off, to* RUDOLPH). Please.

RUDOLPH. Brown, please. (*To* VINCENT.) Has it?

VINCENT. Yeah.

RUDOLPH (*snaps*). You can't love him –

RUDOLPH *clacks some faces down.*

VINCENT (*to* RUDOLPH). Is yours bald?

RUDOLPH. No.

VINCENT *clacks some faces down.*

CORNELIA *appears in a hot-date outfit, carrying two pies on plates.*

CORNELIA. Who's winning?

RUDOLPH. I am for once. Cos I know who it is.

CORNELIA (*to* VINCENT). He'll have misread the rules. Guess Who? Not him.

RUDOLPH. It's Bill, isn't it?

VINCENT. Yeah. Is yours Maria?

MATILDA. She's my French favourite –

RUDOLPH. Too much, too little, too late.

CORNELIA *hands the pies and plates to* VINCENT *and* RUDOLPH.

CORNELIA. Speaking of French, buon appetito, but mind the crumbs on my good carpet.

I've not microwaved you one, Matilda, I didn't want you to exacerbate your selective hyperglycaemia.

MATILDA. I've had some Ready brek.

Over the next section, RUDOLPH *and* VINCENT *eat up on the floor.*

CORNELIA *does a twirl.*

CORNELIA. Feel free to tell me how I look.

VINCENT. You look amazing, Mam.

CORNELIA. Only I'm off to meet Warren this afternoon. And he is more than likely gonna be your new dad at some point. So, it's about time you got over your real dad flitting off with that ten-a-penny slagbag.

VINCENT. Dad died.

CORNELIA. Did he?

RUDOLPH. Yeah.

CORNELIA. Doesn't even ring a bell.

VINCENT. What's he like? Warren.

CORNELIA. He's a shit-hot greengrocer I've been courting for some time now with hands the size of Jupiter and a cock to match.

VINCENT. He sounds a peach.

CORNELIA *curtsys.*

CORNELIA. Thank you.

And I appreciate it might knock you both emotionally so, what I'm proposing, is a family chinky later on tonight, that we whack on that *X Factor* we taped last weekend and all get pissed with Vincent as guest of honour.

Does that sound like a plan?

MATILDA. It sounds perfect.

CORNELIA (*to* RUDOLPH). You score a crate of Foster's from the seven-eleven – (*To* VINCENT.) you pick up the chinky, no cashew nuts for me – (*To* MATILDA.) and you're on Bombay-mix duty, okay?

VINCENT. What time? Only I've got plans myself.

CORNELIA. What plans have you got yourself?

MATILDA. He's meeting Edward.

CORNELIA. Who are you meeting?

RUDOLPH. Edward.

VINCENT. He wants to show me a funeral cake he's working on.

CORNELIA. Do folk have cakes for funerals nowadays, do they?

VINCENT. It's a simple coffin-shaped sponge base but he's stuffed a real raven for aloft the lid.

CORNELIA. How macabre.

Ask him along tonight though, if you like?

RUDOLPH. What for?

CORNELIA. To show you how friendship's done.

CORNELIA *remembers something*.

Shit –

VINCENT. What?

CORNELIA. Sauce. They must be dry as a bone.

CORNELIA *exits into the kitchen*.

RUDOLPH. It's fine.

CORNELIA (*off*). It is not fine, I'll have Child Line on, don't take another bite.

RUDOLPH. Am I invited to come and see Edward with you?

VINCENT. No.

RUDOLPH. Why? What are you doing?

VINCENT. What do you think?

Enter CORNELIA *from the kitchen with two bottles of sauce, plonks them down in front of* VINCENT *and* RUDOLPH.

CORNELIA. I bet it's years since you've had a decent pie, is it, Vincent?

VINCENT. There's an amazing organic pie shop at the end of my street.

CORNELIA. You're not even vegetarian.

RUDOLPH. Vincent's moving out the honeymoon suite and into my room.

CORNELIA. What for?

RUDOLPH. For old time's sake.

(*To* VINCENT.) It's not that he doesn't love the honeymoon suite. It's not filthy. He just loves being back so much that he'd love to be back proper. Like he was. When it was glorious.

CORNELIA. Really?

RUDOLPH. He'd love to be back in the bunk beds. Wouldn't you, Vincent?

CORNELIA. Does he work to commission? This Edward. Only I know exactly what I want for my funeral, if you think he's got it in him to realise it?

VINCENT. What do you want?

CORNELIA. A Viking longboat. With me set ablaze as I sail out to sea like my forefathers before me. Handing myself over to the gods and the crocodiles. To nature, Vincent. Well?

VINCENT. He does more cakes than coffins.

CORNELIA. But could he stretch to a coffin made of a cake?

VINCENT. He is excessively creative. So, maybe –

CORNELIA. Are you listening to this, Rudolph? You wanna take a leaf out your brother's book and make yourself a creative little friend.

(*To* VINCENT.) His best friend's that boxing glove he thinks I don't know he keeps under his pillow.

You will ask him, won't you, Vincent, about tonight?

RUDOLPH. I'm not coming if he is –

CORNELIA. You say it like it's some kind of threat.

RUDOLPH. I'm not.

CORNELIA. Are you deliberately trying to give yourself a nosebleed?

RUDOLPH (*snaps*). I don't want him here.

CORNELIA. And when has what you wanted ever mattered, Rudolph?

RUDOLPH *exits*.

I swear that lad's still to exit puberty.

(*To* VINCENT.) Ignore him. Ask him.

VINCENT. I will.

CORNELIA. Right. (*To herself*.) Wash up. Lipliner. Leave. (*To* VINCENT.) Pass them plates. (*To herself*.) Wash up. Lipliner. Leave.

CORNELIA *takes the plates, exits to the kitchen, the clatter of washing up*.

MATILDA. I finished the last chapter of my novel. Don't tell the others.

VINCENT. Does it have a happy ending?

MATILDA. You'll have to wait and see.

MATILDA *puts her hand to the side of* VINCENT*'s face, holds it*.

Will I play Guess Who? with you?

VINCENT *stands*.

VINCENT. I need to go.

MATILDA. To see your boyfriend?

Enter CORNELIA *from the kitchen.*

CORNELIA (*to* MATILDA). Go and tell sadsack he's to get his arse up that seven-eleven.

VINCENT. I will. I'm heading along now anyway.

CORNELIA. You're a gentleman, a scholar and an acrobat, love.

VINCENT. Enjoy your date, Mam. Where's he taking you this time?

CORNELIA. The town square execution. Rumour has it it's gonna be a fiery one.

VINCENT. Have fun.

VINCENT *kisses* CORNELIA *and exits.*

CORNELIA. See? You wanna get yourself a fitty like me, Matilda.

MATILDA. I've got a fitty. I've got –

VINCENT (*off, shouts*). Rudolph?

CORNELIA. He's no greengrocer, though, is he?

MATILDA. He's my greengrocer –

VINCENT (*off, shouts*). I'm walking along now, if you're coming?

CORNELIA. I doubt he knows his courgettes from his cooking onions.

MATILDA. What does that mean?

CORNELIA. Oral, Matilda. The ballast of many a stable and sustainable relationship, Trisha Goddard's word not mine.

MATILDA. Trisha's husband left her, he was gay.

CORNELIA. Please do not dare swear in this house –

VINCENT (*off, shouts*). This is your last chance.

CORNELIA. And, if Warren ends up back here later, do me a favour and whack a sock in Lucy's mouth –

VINCENT (*off, shouts*). Suit yourself.

CORNELIA. Her whistling puts him in mind of a milkman jauntily going about his rounds and he struggles to maintain an erection.

The front door slams.

Like your Rudolph, I imagine. Though he's his dad to thank for that floppy affliction.

MATILDA. I didn't know Warren'd been here.

CORNELIA. I struggle keep him away.

Now, where've you put my femidoms?

CORNELIA *disappears into the kitchen.*

MATILDA *takes in the balls of rolled wool, violently throws them against the wall, ends up in one almighty and knitted knot as* CORNELIA *re-enters.*

What's happening here?

MATILDA. I dropped them.

CORNELIA. It's becoming a bit of a habit, isn't it, Matilda? But, word from the wise to the not so wise, Lucy's only the way she is cos of what you did.

She's your punishment and Rudolph might've forgiven you, he might've brushed it under that carpet and decided to make the best of his bad lot.

But you monumentally fucked things up –

MATILDA (*snaps*). It wasn't my fault.

CORNELIA *whips out her lipliner, applies it as:*

CORNELIA. Once upon a time there was a family that came to a seaside town.

A family that wanted nothing more than to just see the sea, the dodgems and give candyfloss to their only daughter. A daughter who'd never known such a liberty.

Can you imagine being able to taste candyfloss for the first time again, Matilda?

MATILDA. No.

CORNELIA. But a family that found their only daughter so repulsive and so abhorrent, that they didn't want to take her home again. A family that took another more beautiful child in her place.

A family that left that monster in a guesthouse they hoped would keep her. Care for her. And offer her an ultimately better world than she would ever know anywhere else.

And we did, didn't we? And we have, haven't we?

CORNELIA *takes* MATILDA*'s face in her hands.*

And so I don't want this mess to still be here when we get back. Cos Warren, of anyone, will not tolerate this repulsive side of you.

Okay, love?

MATILDA. Thank you.

CORNELIA *kisses* MATILDA*'s cheek and exits.*

MATILDA *pulls at the mess of wool, rolls them around her fists, into fresh new balls as the lights snap to black.*

Scene Six

Later that night.

'Making Your Mind Up' by Bucks Fizz blares out from a small portable TV and VHS video player downstage centre.

CORNELIA, RUDOLPH, VINCENT *and* MATILDA *are stood in front of it, karaoke microphones in hand, singing along to the* The X Factor, *all pissed.*

Around them is all manner of Chinese-takeaway paraphernalia, dirty plates, empty cans, unopened chopsticks. They sing along to the song.

They all take a seat, wet their whistles, CORNELIA *takes up her knitting as:*

CORNELIA (*to* VINCENT). You'll never watch *The X Factor* in the same light again, will you?

VINCENT. What do you call it?

MATILDA. Sing-along-*The-X-Factor.*

VINCENT. Do we have to do every song?

CORNELIA. We never help the lass with pancreatic cancer.

VINCENT. Why not?

CORNELIA. She puts it on.

RUDOLPH. We should enter next year.

CORNELIA. You'd never get me in that city.

RUDOLPH. It's still worth applying.

CORNELIA. Not when I've told you what Crystal told me earlier.

RUDOLPH. What?

CORNELIA. There was a man once went to that city. Packed his bags and off he went, thinking the streets'd be paved with gold. (*To* VINCENT.) They're not, are they?

VINCENT. No.

CORNELIA. Course not. Still ended up being a right horror show, though. Not ten minutes off that ferry and he was kidnapped by a band of tramps. They whisked him off to an abandoned warehouse in the suburbs somewhere and, Christ, I can't –

CORNELIA *burps, blows it in* RUDOLPH's *face.*

Excuse me, everyone.

RUDOLPH. What did they do to him?

CORNELIA. Tied him to a chair, Rudolph. And one by one whipped out a little set of nail clippers, like the ones I use to do your fingers and toes on a Sunday night.

RUDOLPH. No.

CORNELIA. And hitherto went at him. Those dirty city tramps. Taking turns at nipping little bits off of his body until there was nowt left. Just a pile of crescent-shaped strips of skin littering that abandoned-warehouse floor.

Three days it took in all to strip him back to skeleton. Leaving his eyes until last so he could watch. Crystal was sick in her mouth when she told me.

RUDOLPH. Good God.

VINCENT. Is that even true?

CORNELIA. Why would someone make something like that up?

VINCENT. You said she was an extremist alcoholic.

CORNELIA. You're taking it out of context.

VINCENT. To take everything she said with a sea of salt –

CORNELIA. I said no such thing but that's the city for you, someone saying one thing and you hearing another. It's another world –

I don't know how you've survived as long as you have.

VINCENT. It's nothing like that.

CORNELIA. You don't have to pretend with us, Vincent.

VINCENT. I'm not.

CORNELIA. Morning, noon and night, we've a cavalcade of horror stories blaring out of that telly.

VINCENT. It's called the news.

CORNELIA. You say that, Vincent, but no news is always good news.

RUDOLPH. I don't think it is like that, Mam –

CORNELIA. And how the hell would you know?

RUDOLPH. Vincent's said.

CORNELIA. Three days, Rudolph –

CORNELIA *nips* RUDOLPH*'s arm, he screams, jumps back.*

But you're home now, Vincent. Back by the sea and safe.

VINCENT. Maybe you could come and see for yourself one time?

CORNELIA *points at the TV.*

CORNELIA. If this next one's blind, I'm Uncle Ben.

VINCENT. You can't say that.

CORNELIA. You know what a brilliant TV show I used to love was? *Jimmy's.* All those burnt little faces.

(*To* RUDOLPH.) I used to say that's what'd happen to you if you didn't stop fiddling with yourself, didn't I?

RUDOLPH. You did.

CORNELIA. But, did it stop him? Did it shite.

MATILDA. What I don't understand is how Dannii Minogue makes her hair look like a Cornish pasty. I'd love hair like that.

CORNELIA. Recognise your limitations, Matilda.

VINCENT (*to* CORNELIA). I never saw you in the town square earlier.

CORNELIA. Once you've seen one witch-burning, you've seen them all. I was probably at the back with a hot dog.

VINCENT. We looked everywhere for you. I was hoping you might've introduced me to Warren.

CORNELIA. Of course I'd've introduced you to Warren but, like I say, I never saw you.

MATILDA. Did you have a nice time?

CORNELIA. I'm assuming 'we' is Edward and thee?

VINCENT. Course.

CORNELIA. And where is he now?

VINCENT. He's on a tight deadline with a pineapple upside-down cake.

CORNELIA. Then what a shame it is I missed him this afternoon.

RUDOLPH. Did you tell Warren about him?

CORNELIA. I might've mentioned it.

RUDOLPH. And what did he say?

CORNELIA. That you'd struggle to find a more decent lad.

VINCENT. He is decent.

CORNELIA. That friends like that are hard to come by, Warren's words, not mine.

RUDOLPH. He never said that.

CORNELIA (*to* VINCENT). You wanna cling on to this Edward with both fists. And I imagine it'd be lovely for him to have you around on a potentially permanent basis.

VINCENT. I suppose.

CORNELIA. Packed, though, wasn't it, in the town square, Vincent?

VINCENT. It was dead. Why didn't I see you, Mam?

CORNELIA *continues to knit as:*

CORNELIA (*to* RUDOLPH). When, in the name of all that is holy, do those factory fuckers intend on ringing you about that job?

RUDOLPH. They never said.

CORNELIA. You'd think you'd applied to the FB–fucking-I the way they're dragging it out.

RUDOLPH. I wish I had.

CORNELIA. You've not the ears for night-vision goggles. We'll ring them tomorrow, see what the hold-up is –

RUDOLPH. I don't wanna seem pushy –

CORNELIA. It's not pushy, it's initiative, and, worse case, they've still not decided, it'll be a welcome addition to your pros list. They'll probably offer you it on the spot, over the phone –

RUDOLPH. I don't want to –

CORNELIA. And I'm telling you, you do –

RUDOLPH. But –

CORNELIA. I'll wake you early, we can do it together –

RUDOLPH (*snaps*). No.

CORNELIA. Excuse me but did you just snap at me?

RUDOLPH. I didn't mean to.

CORNELIA. Then I'd thank you never to do it again.

MATILDA. You're losing your rag –

RUDOLPH (*shouts*). I'm not losing my rag.

CORNELIA. I won't warn you again about showing off.

VINCENT. It's not the end of the world if he doesn't get it.

CORNELIA. And why wouldn't he get it?

VINCENT. There's other jobs.

CORNELIA. We're on the bones of our arse, Vincent, in case you hadn't noticed.

VINCENT. Why can't you just reopen the guesthouse?

CORNELIA. And who's gonna manage it, run it, clean it?

VINCENT. Rudolph.

CORNELIA. You could do it, Vincent.

VINCENT. I wouldn't know where to start.

CORNELIA. You cut your teeth dusting those banisters.

VINCENT. I smashed my teeth dusting those banisters.

CORNELIA. I can see you now, meeting and greeting. We could rename it, have a relaunch, get menus made and individual shortbreads.

We could call it Vincent's, Vincent. After you.

VINCENT. I don't think so.

CORNELIA. Cos give people enough of a reason and they always come back. I'll get you a little badge from the cobbler's in the precinct. Manager.

VINCENT. You're drunk –

CORNELIA. On unadulterated excitement. Cos that's it. It's settled.

VINCENT. What about Rudolph?

CORNELIA. He's his factory job as good as promised, he knows his place.

RUDOLPH. If we did reopen, I could do Judy and Punch in the garden to tempt guests in –

CORNELIA. The grown-ups are talking now, Rudolph –

VINCENT (*snaps*). He doesn't want the job, Mam.

CORNELIA. What do you think, Matilda?

MATILDA. Me?

CORNELIA. Yes, you. He's your husband. And won't his time be better spent up that factory?

MATILDA. It's a good job.

CORNELIA (*to* RUDOLPH). See?

MATILDA. I think it's admirable. And that Rudolph could be a proud man. A success. Cos there's opportunities there. But there's opportunities elsewhere, too.

RUDOLPH (*to* CORNELIA). See?

MATILDA. I just want him to be happy, Cornelia.

CORNELIA. Is that right?

MATILDA. For all of us to have some lovely little life that we can call our own. That we can look at and go, that's ours. That we can own.

CORNELIA. Are you quite finished?

MATILDA. I don't know what I'm trying to say –

RUDOLPH. I know exactly what you're trying to say.

CORNELIA. Well, I don't, I'm bored and I'm off to ring Warren about our fantastic new news.

CORNELIA *pulls* MATILDA *up to stand.*

(*To* MATILDA.) You. Bed.

MATILDA. I'm happy just sitting.

CORNELIA. You do nowt but sit.

MATILDA. I do all sorts –

CORNELIA. And don't think I won't be telling my Warren about the show you've made of yourself tonight.

MATILDA. I'm sorry.

CORNELIA. Fingers crossed he's not too pissed to follow it up with a bit of naked phone fun.

MATILDA. I only ever wanted my ears pierced.

CORNELIA. You've lovely ears, come on. We can mull over colour schemes on our way up the stairs –

CORNELIA *leads* MATILDA *through the hall door and up to bed.*

RUDOLPH. I got it.

VINCENT. What?

RUDOLPH. The job.

VINCENT. Congratulations.

RUDOLPH. On my own merit. The first thing I've ever got on that.

VINCENT. When do you start?

RUDOLPH. I turned it down.

VINCENT. Why?

RUDOLPH. Because I'm in love with you.

VINCENT. I love Edward.

RUDOLPH. You're not even gay.

VINCENT. I am. And you're my brother. And you're pissed.

RUDOLPH (*snaps*). I'm not pissed.

VINCENT. You love Matilda. And I love him. Full stop.

> RUDOLPH *launches himself at* VINCENT, *kisses him hard on the lips.*

> VINCENT *pushes him off.*

Stop it.

RUDOLPH. Tell me what really happened. Why you're really here and I could help.

We could fix it together.

Cos I got a job. I'm not stupid after all.

VINCENT. Go to bed.

> RUDOLPH *shakes his head.*

> VINCENT *launches himself at* RUDOLPH, *passionately kisses him.*

> VINCENT *eventually pulls away.*

I'm sorry –

Exit VINCENT.

> *As he slams the hall door, the bulbs of the chandelier blow, leaving the glare of the TV to light* RUDOLPH *who sits, sipping at his can.*

> *The hall door swings open as an elaborately knitted* CROCODILE *enters, sliding along the carpet in sinister silence.*

RUDOLPH *clocks the* CROCODILE, *begins to shake, freezes, as it creeps closer, slow and menacing.*

RUDOLPH *closes his eyes, can't look as it reaches him, sniffs at his feet.*

RUDOLPH (*terrified*). Please?

I'll ring them back. I'll take the job. I promise.

The CROCODILE *slides off into the kitchen.*

RUDOLPH *opens his eyes, breaks down, finishes his drink, facing out, as:*

MATILDA *appears in the hall door, eyes closed, recites from memory:*

MATILDA. Laura had never known love like it.

The speedboat beneath them felt like it was flying to the moon with only two astronauts. Her and Christian. As they zoomed off into space. To wondrous new worlds together.

Christian pressed the shaft of his thick love-wand between her tanned legs. He whispered into her ear that he loved her. That she was the single most perfect thing in this universe.

Laura transformed into stars.

Because Christian was perfect. And she loved him, too. In a way that only Laura could. Like a one-hundred-year-old woman finally spending the money she'd received for her second birthday.

Because Laura's love had been kept locked away until then. In the deepest, darkest room of her heart.

Laura smiled and hung her hand from the side of the speedboat. Her fingertips tickled salty waves as the sun set on her smile.

As Laura waited for Christian to come inside of her.

MATILDA *opens her eyes, smiles at* RUDOLPH.

Thank you.

The lights crocodile-snap to black. Interval.

Scene Seven

'Rhythm is a Dancer' by Snap! blares out.

A spotlight snaps up on the serving hatch, its doors slam open and a knitted MR PUNCH *pops up.*

PUNCH. Hello, boys and girls.

My silly-billy wife has fucked off on a shopping expedition and forgotten to leave me any dinner.

What you think about that?

JUDY (*off*). Mr Punch?

PUNCH. Here's the bitch now –

A knitted JUDY *pops up, cradling a knitted* BABY.

JUDY. I'm so exhausted from doing my make-up and being a mother that I'd appreciate a lie-down from my shopping expedition.

If only there was someone to mind my baby.

Can you mind my baby, Mr Punch?

PUNCH. No.

JUDY. Please?

PUNCH. No.

JUDY. Please?

PUNCH. No.

JUDY. Despite her being so cute, Mr Punch? Despite her inheritance of your gorgeous head, shoulders, knees and nose?

PUNCH (*snaps*). I hate babies and I hate you.

JUDY. Just for five funny minutes?

PUNCH. Only if you promise to suck my cock when you wake up.

JUDY. Why break the habit of a lifetime? Here's the baby. (*To* BABY.) Bye, baby –

JUDY *drops the* BABY *and disappears*.

PUNCH. What the fuck am I meant to do with you?

The BABY *cries*.

Shut up.

The BABY *cries*.

Shut up.

The BABY *cries*.

(*Shouts*.) I'll throw you out to sea like I did with your brother.

The BABY *stops crying*.

That's a good baby girl.

Little angel. Little girl.

MR PUNCH *picks up the* BABY.

(*Sings*.)
Lucy Locket lost her pocket,
Kitty Fisher found it,
Not a penny in her purse,
But a ribbon round it –

MR PUNCH *suddenly stops, gasps*.

Did you just bite me, baby?

The BABY *shakes its head*.

(*Snaps*.) You fucking did –

MR PUNCH *repeatedly bangs* BABY*'s head against the wooden door of the serving hatch,* BABY *wailing as:*

(*Shouts*.) Bad baby.

Bad, bad, bad, bad, bad baby –

MR PUNCH *continues until the* BABY *stops crying*.

That's right. That's better. Silly, silent baby. Stupid baby.

MR PUNCH *places the* BABY *solemnly in the centre of the hatch, has the smallest second of regret, head down.*

Oh, dear. Broken baby. All my fault –

A knitted MR CROCODILE *pops up.* MR PUNCH *screams.*

CROCODILE. What did you do that for?

PUNCH. I didn't do anything. She's fine. Watch her dance –

MR PUNCH *picks up the* BABY, *animates her.*

See?

CROCODILE. Drop the baby.

MR PUNCH *drops the baby.*

Close your eyes.

PUNCH. I don't want to –

CROCODILE. Turn around.

MR PUNCH *turns around.*

PUNCH. What are you gonna do?

CROCODILE. I've an empty, echoing stomach. And I'm gonna gobble you up whole –

MR PUNCH *screams as* MR CROCODILE *snaps at him, chases him down into the dark.*

Lighting change.

The next morning. VINCENT *stands in the doorway, head to toe in flour.*

VINCENT. Are you in there?

RUDOLPH (*off*). You know I am.

VINCENT. What you doing?

RUDOLPH (*off*). I wanted to do one last show.

VINCENT. Can I see?

RUDOLPH (*off*). No.

VINCENT. I could do the crocodile.

RUDOLPH. (*off*) It's a new start.

Enter RUDOLPH *with his knitted Punch and Judy puppets.*

You look like a ghost.

VINCENT. Me and Edward had a fight.

Over the next section, RUDOLPH *places his puppets in a carrier bag, as if laying out the dead.*

RUDOLPH. Do you want to go for a drink tonight?

VINCENT. Where's Mam?

RUDOLPH. Upstairs on the phone to Warren.

VINCENT. Have you met him?

RUDOLPH. They're having another tapas night up The Cherry Blossom. Are you a fan of tapas?

VINCENT. I don't think that's a good idea.

RUDOLPH. It is a good idea. It's my idea. And I love tapas.

VINCENT. Matilda said he's been here plenty but she's never seen him.

RUDOLPH. It starts at eight with sangria from half seven. So if we're there for six we'll be sure to get a seat –

VINCENT. Have you seen him, Rudolph?

RUDOLPH. He sells magic mushrooms to kids.

VINCENT. Who says?

RUDOLPH (*snaps*). Everyone says.

RUDOLPH *ties the top of the carrier bag, forces the air out.*

VINCENT. What are you gonna do with them?

RUDOLPH. Was that a 'yes' to tonight?

VINCENT. I'm seeing Edward.

RUDOLPH. I thought you'd had a fight.

VINCENT. We have.

RUDOLPH. That's surely the end of that, then?

VINCENT. No.

RUDOLPH. I passed his shop before. I'd wondered about those cakes you're always banging on about –

VINCENT. You didn't –

RUDOLPH. He looked devastated, Vincent. Even before your fall-out.

VINCENT. What did he say?

RUDOLPH. We didn't speak. Should I have gone in and told him you're cheating on him? Only you said to stay away.

VINCENT. I never said that.

RUDOLPH. You should know what's wrong with him. He's your gay boyfriend.

VINCENT. No one likes a smart-arse, Rudolph.

RUDOLPH. I'll go and see him now, if you want? Tell him what's what. I'm not scared –

VINCENT. I don't want.

RUDOLPH. Was the fight about me?

VINCENT. About when I leave.

RUDOLPH. If he loves you, he should surely want the best for you.

VINCENT. He does.

RUDOLPH. By viciously attacking you with flour?

VINCENT. I asked for it –

RUDOLPH. You could've lost an eye, Vincent.

VINCENT. I'm gonna apologise –

RUDOLPH. It should be him saying sorry –

VINCENT. I want to take him to the city. To ask him to come home with me.

RUDOLPH. You can't.

VINCENT. We'll see in Lucy's birthday and then leave.

RUDOLPH. He's not welcome.

VINCENT. He's welcome with me.

Cos his cakes'll be applauded there. Their opulence. Their originality, each and every one of them, one of a kind –

RUDOLPH (*snaps*). They're ugly.

That's not fair.

VINCENT. I know he'll make it all okay again.

RUDOLPH. I can be original, too. I can be interesting and impressive, too.

You see that in me, don't you? Cos I can't breathe here, Vincent. I try to. But it won't come.

You of anyone must understand that. Folk struggling to see you. So hard they never really ever see you.

You must've felt that. Cos it's not too late to keep your promise, Vincent.

VINCENT. Whatever you think you are. You're not.

You're hardly rocket science, Rudolph. Or anything remotely special.

RUDOLPH *smashes his bag of puppets off the wall, breaks down.*

Enter CORNELIA.

CORNELIA. Rudolph?

RUDOLPH. What?

CORNELIA. All I can smell is crab.

VINCENT. He was just reminiscing.

CORNELIA. Well, reminisce this. Out. Now.

CORNELIA *snatches* RUDOLPH*'s bag of puppets, slams them in a cupboard as* RUDOLPH *exits.*

CORNELIA *grabs an air freshener from the kitchen, sprays the room.*

Warren's moving in.

VINCENT. When?

CORNELIA. He's popping round tomorrow to meet everyone. You will be here, won't you, Vincent? I'd love him to meet my pride and joy.

VINCENT. Course.

CORNELIA. My manager.

Cos this is just the start of me. I'll be wearing pencil skirts and a spiral perm before you know it.

VINCENT. I'm really looking forward to meeting him.

CORNELIA. And he's so very looking forward to meeting you. I've told him all about you, your magnetic personality, your creative streak and that CBBC thing that was prematurely cancelled where you did sign language to a beanbag beef burger.

VINCENT. It's Lucy's party tomorrow.

CORNELIA. She'll not mind. But we'll have to spruce the place up. I don't want him thinking we live like pigs, not that we do.

VINCENT. But I thought he'd been here?

CORNELIA. Not with a view to being a full-time resident. Mind, it took me a while to talk him round, he's incredibly attached to that two-man tent of his but, what can I say, I say jump, he says, how high?

He also said to remind Rudolph to ring about that job.

VINCENT. Do they know each other?

CORNELIA. No, but they're like two peas in a pod. And Warren's literally beside himself to be his new dad.

VINCENT. I'll remind him to ring when I see him.

CORNELIA. What he wants with those puppets is beyond me, I swear he's regressing.

VINCENT. What will you do with them?

CORNELIA. They're going straight off the end of that pier to the crocodiles.

VINCENT. Is that fair?

CORNELIA. Since when was life fair to any of us, Vincent?

CORNELIA *sits and knits as:*

I'll tell you what I want for Warren's arrival. I want it just how it used to be when you were kids, when this guesthouse was the talk of this town. Like it will be again and rightly so –

You will help me, won't you?

VINCENT. Course.

CORNELIA. We'll start by sugar-soaping these walls. And we'll need a colourful curtain up so he can't see into that kitchen, unless our Matilda's time to bleach the lino.

Cos you know it's true love, don't you, Vincent, when you fear that any second it could be snatched away from you.

VINCENT. How did you meet him?

CORNELIA. Me and Warren met forty years ago up that funfair. Long before your dad, before you and even Rudolph. And I've thought of him all that time and he's thought of me, he says.

You could say we were each other's first love.

All we did was share a waltzer, each the one too many to fit in with our friends.

And then, last year, he spun back into my life. Just as quick and exhilarating up that precinct. I knew exactly who he was straight away, him me.

We'll be one big happy family, won't we? Cos we can be just like we were. Like when you pair were kids and people would line that street for just a peek inside these four walls.

VINCENT. Course we can, Mam.

CORNELIA. And you will stay, won't you, Vincent?

Cos I couldn't bear it if you left me again so soon with everything just finally falling into place for me.

VINCENT. I'll make a start on these walls, will I?

CORNELIA. That's my kind-hearted, my beautiful boy. My manager.

CORNELIA *furiously knits as the lights snap to black.*

Scene Eight

Later that night.

MATILDA *and* VINCENT *are sat on the sofa, they're drinking wine.*

VINCENT. I can't find him.

MATILDA. Edward?

VINCENT. He's not been into work. I asked. But they've heard neither hide nor hair from him either.

MATILDA. He's probably still upset from the fight. You're very beautiful, Vincent. It can't be easy.

VINCENT. Probably. Yeah.

MATILDA. I sold my novel.

VINCENT. Sorry?

MATILDA. They've offered me a ten-thousand-pound advance.

VINCENT. Ten –

MATILDA. Thousand-pound advance, Vincent. I know.

The librarian helped me type it up and fax it to what's called a publisher.

VINCENT. And they bought it?

MATILDA. They read it straight away.

VINCENT. Congratulations.

MATILDA. The lady who rang said that she felt like Laura from the very first page.

And isn't that good? That I could do that to a woman?

VINCENT. It's unbelievable.

MATILDA. It's true.

VINCENT. I believe you.

MATILDA. Sorry.

VINCENT. Don't apologise.

VINCENT *raises his glass*.

To you.

MATILDA. To me.

They chink and drink.

VINCENT. We sound like a couple of Chuckle Brothers.

MATILDA. I chuckle feel like one.

She wants me to go and meet her.

VINCENT. When?

MATILDA. I've not said anything to Rudolph or Cornelia yet.

She wants me to go to the city.

VINCENT. You've got to.

MATILDA. What about Lucy?

VINCENT. Rudolph can look after her for once.

MATILDA. She did say that I'd have to make some changes.

VINCENT. When does she want to meet you?

MATILDA. Monday.

VINCENT. Go.

MATILDA. There's stuff spelt wrong in it. Cos I never properly finished school.

And Malia's a place I'd never even experienced apart from in that documentary. But it changed, Vincent. To a completely different place. A new one.

She called it a paradise. Like the bird.

VINCENT. It sounds beautiful.

MATILDA. As beautiful as Edward even? Sorry.

VINCENT. I'm asking him to come home with me.

MATILDA. To the city?

VINCENT. I know it'll be better with him there.

MATILDA. Do you think he'll go?

VINCENT. I think he will. And it feels right. It feels so perfect that he shouldn't be here in exactly the same way that neither should I.

MATILDA. Then everything will be okay.

VINCENT. But where is he?

Enter RUDOLPH, *he's pissed.*

RUDOLPH. Her penguins are out again. I tried to p-p-p-pick one up to show you but I just smashed it on its head.

RUDOLPH *plonks himself down between* MATILDA *and* VINCENT.

MATILDA. Where've you been?

RUDOLPH. I went for one little drink and I've had a wonderful time, thank you.

Is that wine?

MATILDA. I only had a sip.

RUDOLPH. Been boring you sideways about Edward, has he?

MATILDA. No.

VINCENT. Grow the fuck up.

RUDOLPH *puts his arm around* VINCENT.

RUDOLPH (*to* MATILDA). Love job, apparently. What do you make of that?

MATILDA. I think it's lovely.

RUDOLPH (*to* VINCENT). You wanna be ashamed of yourself.

VINCENT. I'm ashamed of you.

RUDOLPH. But I'm not the gender bender, am I?

VINCENT *shrugs* RUDOLPH*'s arm away, stands.*

What?

VINCENT. You're embarrassing yourself.

RUDOLPH. I was only making conversation.

RUDOLPH *puts his arm around* MATILDA, *moves in for a snog, she retracts.*

(*Snaps.*) What?

MATILDA. You stink of drink.

RUDOLPH. And you stink of shite but you don't hear me complaining –

VINCENT. Come on –

RUDOLPH (*shouts*). 'Come on', what –

RUDOLPH *punches the back of the sofa, just missing* MATILDA*'s head.*

Come where, Vincent?

VINCENT. I think you should go to bed.

RUDOLPH. I've had one drink all night, alright?

VINCENT. Alright. Would you like a glass of wine?

MATILDA. Is that wise?

RUDOLPH (*mocking*). 'Is that wise'? (*To* MATILDA.) What fucker asked you?

VINCENT. Do you want one?

RUDOLPH. I'll have a can. If you can lift it with your limp wrists.

VINCENT takes a can from the fridge, unclips it, hands it to RUDOLPH.

RUDOLPH takes a drink, picks his nose, wipes it on MATILDA's arm.

The sound of LUCY whistling from upstairs.

Who rattled her cage?

MATILDA stands.

MATILDA. She's excited for her party.

RUDOLPH. And how on earth can you fathom what does and does not excite that creature?

Go on, then.

MATILDA. You go.

RUDOLPH. No. You go.

MATILDA looks to VINCENT.

What are you looking at him for?

MATILDA. It's your turn, Rudolph.

RUDOLPH (*to* VINCENT). Have you put her up to this?

VINCENT. What?

RUDOLPH. Thinking for her-fucking-self. (*To* MATILDA.) Well?

VINCENT. You're a cunt.

RUDOLPH. I'm surprised you know what one looks like.

How is the boyfriend? Where is Edward?

The sound of LUCY whistling from upstairs.

(*To* MATILDA.) Well?

MATILDA *sits down*.

RUDOLPH *laughs, a mix of disbelief and defeat*.

(*To* VINCENT.) You can't just leave me here.

VINCENT. This is your home –

RUDOLPH. Home is where the heart is –

VINCENT. You're a joke –

RUDOLPH. Aye, and you're the fucking punchline.

The sound of LUCY *whistling from upstairs*.

(*Snaps, to* MATILDA.) I won't tell you again –

VINCENT. Don't talk to her like that –

RUDOLPH. She doesn't even care –

VINCENT. She does nowt but –

RUDOLPH. Then you wanna take a leaf out of her book –

VINCENT. And what?

RUDOLPH. Care more. About me.

Did you even miss me? Think about me in all this time?

Cos I'm still here. Still that lad you left behind –

VINCENT. I don't even recognise you, Rudolph.

RUDOLPH (*shouts, to* MATILDA). Will you just fucking go?

MATILDA *doesn't budge*.

MATILDA. Warren's moving in.

RUDOLPH. Don't lie.

VINCENT. He's coming round tomorrow to meet us.

RUDOLPH. I won't be here.

VINCENT. You have to.

RUDOLPH. Cos we could go now, couldn't we? Me and you.

VINCENT. She wants the place tidied –

RUDOLPH. It's not too late, there's buses, I've checked –

VINCENT. Wants it like it was when we were little –

RUDOLPH. The fucking Brady Bunch now, are we?

I'm sorry. I've had one drink. I'll behave. I promise.

I could help you pack your things? Pay for the bus, my treat. Will I get you your coat?

VINCENT. I can't go with you, Rudolph.

RUDOLPH. You're no better than me, you know.

You think you are but you're not. It's in everything you do. Everything you say. That look. Poor Rudolph and his shitty knitted-puppet show.

But that's all you do. I see you. In that city. On this telly. We're as alike as we ever were.

We've just different puppets, Vincent.

VINCENT. I never thought I was better than you.

RUDOLPH. I hate you.

I actually physically fucking hate you.

RUDOLPH *goes for* VINCENT, *a punch-up ensues as they crash into the coffee table, over the sofa and end up in a bit of a wrestle downstage centre.*

MATILDA *screams, covers her eyes, terrified.*

RUDOLPH *pins* VINCENT *down, forces a snog onto him, pins his hands with one hand, goes for his belt buckle with the other.* RUDOLPH *suddenly stops, exits as the lights snap to black.*

Scene Nine

The next night.

The room has been tidied, there's bunting, streamers and balloons. The dining table is awash with buffet, tucked away under a knitted white blanket.

RUDOLPH *and* MATILDA *are sat up straight on the sofa, in matching knitted jumpers, their names across the front in a garish colourful font.*

CORNELIA *enters from the kitchen, she's dressed to kill.*

CORNELIA. Buffet, bunting and a blistering soundtrack ready on the record player. I think we might be set.

MATILDA. Should I pop Lucy's presents out?

CORNELIA. It's hardly her day, Matilda.

MATILDA. It's her birthday.

CORNELIA. How old this time?

MATILDA. Two.

CORNELIA. And still lacking enough puff to blow out a candle.

MATILDA. She smiled the other day.

CORNELIA. She's no doubt cottoned on to the fact that she's got a new grandparent.

MATILDA. Who?

CORNELIA. Warren. Bonehead. He'll be here any minute.

MATILDA. Will I pop them out?

CORNELIA. What have you got her?

MATILDA. An Etch A Sketch and a flute.

CORNELIA. And what good's that to the likes of her?

MATILDA. It's the vibrations. I saw a documentary on a profoundly deaf girl who got to grade eight clarinet in four months. She's with the London Symphony Orchestra now.

CORNELIA. You and your bloody documentaries. Someone wants to make one on you.

MATILDA. There's nothing worth documenting about me.

RUDOLPH. That's the most sensible thing you've said all week.

CORNELIA. Sit up straight, Rudolph, and try not to spit so much when you speak.

RUDOLPH *sits up, wipes his mouth as* MATILDA *takes several gift bags from behind the sofa, places them on the table behind the buffet as:*

MATILDA. I'll pop them over here where they're no trouble. We can open them once Warren's gone.

CORNELIA. That's the point though, Matilda, he'll not be gone, he's moving in. He'll be here any minute.

MATILDA. Right. Sorry.

CORNELIA. What's that in your hair?

MATILDA. Mascara. Cos I was thinking once we reopen Vincent's, I could do an Ann Summers party for the guests. Cos I think I could be really good at it eventually.

RUDOLPH. No one else does.

MATILDA. I could be sexier, Rudolph.

CORNELIA. Park your arse, Matilda, you're worrying the buffet.

MATILDA. Why's there a blanket over it?

MATILDA *makes to lift the blanket from the buffet.*

CORNELIA *races over and slaps* MATILDA*'s hand.*

CORNELIA. To stop it from sweating. Sit.

MATILDA. Sorry.

CORNELIA. You can have some when he gets here. I want him to see it in all its glory before I let you greedy gannets loose.

MATILDA. I can't wait.

CORNELIA. Button it. He'll be here any minute.

MATILDA sits.

Who wants a little Buck's Fizz to get us in the zone?

RUDOLPH. I'll have a can.

CORNELIA. Please.

RUDOLPH. Please.

MATILDA. Just a little one for me, please –

Exit CORNELIA to the kitchen.

CORNELIA (*off*). Someone ring Vincent and see where he's got to?

RUDOLPH. I will.

RUDOLPH stands.

MATILDA. Did you get Lucy anything?

RUDOLPH. That's your department.

MATILDA. It's okay. I put both names on the presents.

RUDOLPH. Why when she can't see to read?

MATILDA. I thought it was a nice touch.

RUDOLPH. She'll think you're taking the piss.

CORNELIA (*off*). Earth to morons. Someone ring Vincent. Warren'll be here any minute –

CORNELIA returns with a fistful of drinks.

The sound of the front door slamming.

(*Off.*) Never mind, this'll be him now.

CORNELIA hands out the drinks, they chink and drink.

Enter VINCENT, he's visibly upset.

Where the blazes have you been?

VINCENT. Edward's parents and they've not seen him either.

CORNELIA. Prince Edward?

VINCENT. My Edward.

CORNELIA. Never mind. Get your jumper on, we're just waiting on Warren, he'll be here any minute.

RUDOLPH. He's four hours late –

CORNELIA. Thank you, Rudolph.

VINCENT. Are you deaf? He's a missing person.

CORNELIA. He's probably just lost track of time up the rock shop, now blow your nose and swift upstairs to freshen up.

VINCENT. I don't want to blow my nose. I've been looking all day.

It's been twenty-four hours.

CORNELIA. Look at you in a right state. But friends come and go, Vincent, stepfathers are for life. Here –

CORNELIA *whips a name jumper from her knitting bag, undresses* VINCENT*, pops him into it as:*

MATILDA. What did his mam and dad say?

VINCENT. They've not seen him.

RUDOLPH. Maybe Warren knows something?

CORNELIA. What are you saying that for?

RUDOLPH. He did say you'd struggle to find a more decent lad.

MATILDA. Are you alright, Vincent?

CORNELIA (*to* RUDOLPH). I'll be sure to ask him when he arrives –

VINCENT (*to* MATILDA). Not really –

VINCENT *breaks down.* MATILDA *sits him down.*

CORNELIA. That's it, love, you tend to him.

VINCENT (*to* RUDOLPH). You don't know anything, do you?

RUDOLPH. I was told to stay away, Vincent.

MATILDA. Where have you checked?

VINCENT. Everywhere.

CORNELIA. Well, there's little to no point in upsetting the rest of us, is there?

MATILDA. I'm sure he's fine, Vincent.

CORNELIA. Buck's Fizz to take the edge off?

VINCENT. Please.

MATILDA. Have mine.

> MATILDA *hands* VINCENT *her drink and gets herself another, brings the bottle through, tops everyone up.*

VINCENT. Where's Warren?

CORNELIA. He'll be here any minute.

MATILDA. He's four hours late –

CORNELIA. Thank you, Matilda.

VINCENT. Maybe he's not coming.

CORNELIA. Of course he's bloody coming, why wouldn't he come?

VINCENT. I don't know –

CORNELIA (*snaps*). No, you don't know.

> CORNELIA *composes herself, finds a maternal bone in her body, clings onto* VINCENT.

I am so very sorry about your missing friend, Vincent.

VINCENT. I just can't think where he is.

CORNELIA. Are you thinking what I'm thinking?

VINCENT. I doubt it.

CORNELIA. Well, we all know one little lady equipped to locate the baker of cakes. Someone who knows everything about everyone.

RUDOLPH. Not Lucy –

CORNELIA. Ten team points to the dubious-looking gentleman in the jumper.

(*To* MATILDA.) You, upstairs and get her. We'll play that whistling parlour game she lives for –

RUDOLPH. She'll be asleep –

MATILDA. She's not.

CORNELIA. I was hoping we'd get a round of this in –

RUDOLPH. I said, no –

CORNELIA. Are you really gonna deny that creature her first and last chance to light up a room? On her birthday of all days?

RUDOLPH. No.

MATILDA. I'll go and get her.

CORNELIA. Wait till you see her, Vincent. She certainly gives Paul Daniels a run for his funny money –

MATILDA *exits*.

(*To* RUDOLPH.) Dim the big light, you know what her eyes are like.

RUDOLPH. She's blind.

CORNELIA. I won't tell you again.

RUDOLPH *dims the lights*.

VINCENT. I might just have one last walk along the seafront –

CORNELIA. You most certainly will not. Cos for once I need you. And for once you're actually here. So sit quiet and drink your drink –

VINCENT. I'm just so worried –

CORNELIA (*snaps*). You should be worried about me.

VINCENT. There's nothing wrong with you.

Enter MATILDA *carrying* LUCY, *a two-year-old shape beneath a blanket, we should never see her.*

MATILDA *places* LUCY *centre stage, they all gather in a circle around her.*

CORNELIA. Hello, Lucy, love –

LUCY *whistles a jaunty 'hello'.*

(*To* LUCY.) One for 'yes' and two for 'no', as per, okay?

LUCY *whistles once.*

Who wants to kick her off?

VINCENT. What are we meant to be doing?

CORNELIA. Ask her absolutely anything and she'll tell you the truth, it's her one redeeming feature.

VINCENT. I don't feel comfortable with this –

CORNELIA. It's only a bit of fun and she's glad of the company.

I'll start her off with a simple one. (*To* LUCY.) Am I in love with Warren, Lucy?

LUCY *whistles once.*

That's a given, isn't it?

(*To* LUCY.) And are you made up that your Uncle Vincent's finally come home to us?

LUCY *whistles once.*

I think you've got a fan here.

RUDOLPH (*to* LUCY). Do you know why he's really come home?

LUCY *whistles once.*

CORNELIA. No one needs a reason to come home, Rudolph. Least of all this pride and joy.

MATILDA. Your mam's right –

RUDOLPH (*to* LUCY). Is she right, Lucy? Does he even want to be here?

LUCY *whistles twice.*

CORNELIA. She's in a micey mood, take her back to the attic.

VINCENT. Wait –

CORNELIA (*to* VINCENT). Not now, Vincent. (*To*
MATILDA.) Now, Matilda –

VINCENT (*to* LUCY). Has Rudolph said something to Edward?

LUCY *whistles once.*

I asked you, you said no –

CORNELIA. And you had the audacity to finger my Warren –

MATILDA. What have you said?

RUDOLPH. I've never even met him.

VINCENT. You said you saw him and he was devastated –

CORNELIA. I knew this was a good idea –

RUDOLPH (*snaps*). I've said nothing.

CORNELIA. That's not what Lucy's led to believe –

VINCENT (*snaps*). What did you say?

I just wanna know he's okay.

MATILDA (*to* LUCY). Is Edward okay, Lucy?

LUCY *whistles once.*

VINCENT. Then where is he?

CORNELIA. You know the rules, Vincent, only yes or no
questions.

RUDOLPH (*to* LUCY). Do you know why Vincent was fired?

LUCY *whistles once.*

VINCENT. This is cruel.

LUCY *whistles once.*

MATILDA. Vincent?

VINCENT. I resigned.

RUDOLPH (*to* LUCY). Did he do something wrong?

CORNELIA. Don't give her any more clues –

RUDOLPH (*to* LUCY). Did he?

> LUCY *whistles once.*

> The plot thickens –

CORNELIA. He left because he wanted to.

VINCENT. I didn't do anything.

CORNELIA. Of course you didn't, he's only jealous, ignore him –

RUDOLPH. CBBC don't just fire people for nothing.

CORNELIA. I'm sure they had a valid reason.

RUDOLPH (*to* LUCY). That's the point though, isn't it, Lucy?

> LUCY *whistles once.*

> They had a reason.

> LUCY *whistles once.*

VINCENT. Pending investigation.

RUDOLPH. Not so fucking perfect now, are you? Golden boy.

> (*To* CORNELIA.) See, Mam? He's only come home cos he had to. Cos he was forced to. Cos he was forced out.

> (*To* LUCY.) He's hiding, isn't he, Lucy?

> LUCY *whistles once.*

VINCENT. Leave her alone.

> LUCY *whistles once.*

RUDOLPH. What was the reason?

CORNELIA. You're gonna burn her out, give her a general knowledge –

RUDOLPH. We'll find out somehow. And what better way than the whistling game –

CORNELIA. It certainly shits all over Twister.

RUDOLPH (*to* VINCENT). Well?

It's you or Lucy. Either way, we're finding out.

MATILDA (*to* LUCY). Was it kids, Lucy?

LUCY *whistles twice*.

VINCENT. Why would it be kids?

MATILDA. I don't know –

RUDOLPH. It could've been –

VINCENT. I would never –

MATILDA. I'm sorry.

RUDOLPH. Not so thick as thieves now, are you? You pair.

VINCENT. Really, Matilda? Kids?

RUDOLPH. That Edward must be barely legal –

VINCENT. I thought you'd never met him –

CORNELIA. Warren said you'd struggle to find a more decent
    lad, you can ask him yourself, he'll be here any minute –

VINCENT. Tell me what you said to him –

LUCY *whistles twice*.

Tell me where he is, Rudolph –

LUCY *whistles twice*.

(*To* LUCY, *snaps*.) I'm not talking to you.

MATILDA. There's no need to snap at her.

RUDOLPH. I've told you. I don't know.

(*To* LUCY.) Was it drugs, Lucy?

VINCENT (*to* LUCY). Did Rudolph get his job?

LUCY *whistles once*.

CORNELIA. You got it?

RUDOLPH (*to* LUCY). Was it drink?

VINCENT (*to* LUCY). He definitely got it?

LUCY *whistles once.*

CORNELIA. Well, why didn't you say?

MATILDA. That's brilliant, Rudolph –

RUDOLPH. It's still his turn – (*To* LUCY.) what did he do, Lucy?

CORNELIA. You were waiting for Warren, weren't you? That's so thoughtful, come here –

CORNELIA *hugs* RUDOLPH, *squeezes him like he's going out of fashion.*

I'm so proud of you –

CORNELIA *takes* RUDOLPH'*s face in her hands, beams, as proud as punch, it means the world to him.*

I can't tell you how much –

VINCENT (*to* LUCY). Did he turn it down, Lucy?

LUCY *whistles once.*

He fucked it off. He turned it down, Mam –

CORNELIA *grabs* RUDOLPH'*s ears as:*

CORNELIA. Rudolph?

RUDOLPH. I didn't want it –

CORNELIA *twists* RUDOLPH'*s ears as:*

CORNELIA. But I wanted it, I wanted it for you –

CORNELIA *pulls* RUDOLPH'*s head down to her knee, kicks at him, slaps him, as he breaks down.*

VINCENT *eventually pulls* CORNELIA *away, she's out of breath.*

(*Screams.*) You. Stupid. Fucking. Fuck –

RUDOLPH (*shouts*). I'm not stupid –

CORNELIA. Oh, you are, Rudolph. You are the thickest fucking thing in this world.

LUCY *whistles twice.*

RUDOLPH. See?

CORNELIA (*snaps*). Enough.

VINCENT. Mam?

MATILDA. Will I take her back up to the attic?

CORNELIA. Wait.

(*To* LUCY.) Vincent will stay with us for ever, won't he, Lucy?

LUCY *whistles once.*

Thank you.

VINCENT. I don't know –

CORNELIA. Home is where the heart is, Vincent. So, surely that's right here, is it not?

RUDOLPH. It's not. It's with Edward.

CORNELIA *necks her drink, composes herself, takes a deep breath.*

CORNELIA. Did you hear that?

RUDOLPH. Mam?

CORNELIA. The doorbell. He's here.

VINCENT. I didn't hear anything.

CORNELIA. Of course you did. You all did. Pull yourselves together and I'll go and get him. I told you Warren'd be here any minute.

Stand in a line like the von Trapps –

Exit CORNELIA *as* VINCENT, RUDOLPH *and* MATILDA *line up in front of the sofa.*

MATILDA. Vincent?

VINCENT. Leave me alone.

CORNELIA *enters with a life-sized and elaborately knitted man, he has 'Warren' emblazoned across his chest, a beard, knitted shoes, hair and ears.*

CORNELIA. Well, say hello, then.

VINCENT. Sorry?

CORNELIA. You're being rude. Say hello.

RUDOLPH. Hello.

CORNELIA. That's better. This is Warren. And Warren says, 'Hi, guys.'

Why don't we let him sit down and take you all in properly?

CORNELIA *plonks Warren down on the sofa, sits next to him, takes his hand.*

VINCENT. Mam?

CORNELIA. Don't call me that in front of Warren, I've told him I'm twenty-two.

He's laughing his head off here. Private joke.

VINCENT. What are you doing?

CORNELIA. Perhaps Warren would like to be offered some buffet, Matilda?

MATILDA. Can I interest you in some buffet, Warren?

CORNELIA. Probably just a plate of pretzels. He's insatiable for anything with a high salt content.

MATILDA *removes the blanket from the buffet, it's all knitted.*

MATILDA. Would you like some, Cornelia?

CORNELIA. No. I'm a textbook slug when it comes to salt.

MATILDA *plates up some buffet.*

CORNELIA *nods at* RUDOLPH *to make an effort with Warren.*

RUDOLPH. Why were you so late, Warren?

CORNELIA. He happened upon a road-traffic accident and was required to resuscitate a dozen or more fatalities.

LUCY *whistles once.* CORNELIA *nods at* VINCENT *to do the same.*

VINCENT. Are you a paramedic?

LUCY *whistles once.*

CORNELIA. He's his St John's Ambulance level one and never goes anywhere without a fistful of Barley Sugars. Isn't that right?

Warren says that's correct and thank you for asking, Vincent.

MATILDA *hands the buffet out,* CORNELIA *pretends to feed Warren.*

How nice is this? Everything I've ever dreamed of and more.

RUDOLPH. Would you like a drink, Warren?

CORNELIA. He'd like a whiskey and cream soda, thank you.

RUDOLPH. I don't think we've got any whiskey.

CORNELIA. He's expressing severe disappointment at that, Rudolph.

RUDOLPH. I could nip to the seven-eleven?

CORNELIA. I said he was a treasure, didn't I, Warren? Said you'd get on like a house on fire and rightly so. Two peas, one pod. (*To* RUDOLPH.) You're a rare gem, Rudolph.

RUDOLPH. Does anyone else want anything while I'm out?

VINCENT *and* MATILDA *shake their heads.*

I won't be long.

CORNELIA. There's money on the side.

RUDOLPH. I've got money, I'll not be long.

Exit RUDOLPH.

CORNELIA. Well, here we are. The final puzzle piece firmly in place. One big happy family.

I'm feeling a bit tipsy, is anyone else?

VINCENT. I'm feeling really tipsy.

MATILDA. Would you like to hold Lucy, Warren?

CORNELIA. Warren's actually allergic to dogs, Matilda. So, if you'd kindly take it back upstairs –

MATILDA. But –

CORNELIA. Would you really have him break out in hives on his first night in his new home?

MATILDA. Course not.

CORNELIA. Goodbye then.

    MATILDA *scoops up* LUCY, *exits*.

VINCENT. I really should go and find Edward –

CORNELIA. Wait –

    CORNELIA *stands*.

VINCENT. Mam?

CORNELIA. I don't want to make a scene. And I won't entertain tears.

But I would just like to say. In the company of those that I hold dearest. That you, Warren, have made me the happiest woman alive.

Forty long years I've waited for today. And here you are. At last. Mine all mine –

    CORNELIA *snatches her palm to her stomach, catches her breath*.

VINCENT. Are you alright?

CORNELIA. It's just the butterflies. They've been such a long time coming.

    The lights snap to black.

Scene Ten

Later that night.

CORNELIA *is breaking her heart on the sofa as* VINCENT *enters.*

VINCENT. What's going on?

CORNELIA *sits* VINCENT *down, takes his hands.*

CORNELIA. I've some terrible news for you.

VINCENT. Is it Edward?

CORNELIA. It's Rudolph.

VINCENT. Is he back from the seven-eleven?

CORNELIA. He's not at the seven-eleven. I've just come from there.

VINCENT. I thought you were showing Warren the garden?

CORNELIA. No. I've been to the seven-eleven. There's been a fire.

VINCENT. At the seven-eleven?

CORNELIA. On the seaside.

VINCENT. Where?

CORNELIA. Rudolph's ice-cream van.

VINCENT. How?

CORNELIA. Mrs Sausage from the seven-eleven only had half a story when we got there. But me and Warren walked down to see for ourselves and –

VINCENT. And?

CORNELIA. The emergency services were there. Vomiting onto their steel-toecapped pumps at what there was to behold.

VINCENT. We can always find him another one –

CORNELIA. You're not listening, Vincent.

They were dragging out a charred skeleton as we arrived.

VINCENT. No, they weren't.

CORNELIA. I can only assume Rudolph's wandered down for one last look on his way to the seven-eleven. In lieu of his upcoming role at the cardboard factory. That someone's locked him in and he's burned alive, writhing in agony the lads assured us –

VINCENT. You're lying.

CORNELIA. Why would a mother ever lie to her only son, Vincent?

VINCENT. I'm going down there –

CORNELIA. There's nothing you can do for him now, love. He was as black as the ace of spades.

VINCENT. What happened?

CORNELIA. Like I say, some cruel bastards more than likely bolted him in and, I'm assuming, doused the area with petrol, lit a lighter and the rest, as the say, is horrible history.

VINCENT. I want to see him.

CORNELIA. I wouldn't. He was quite the frightful sight. And that's me being kind.

But if it's any consolation, any silver lining to this emotionally crippling night, it's that he went the way he would've wanted –

VINCENT. By being burnt alive?

CORNELIA. In his van. With his only true friendship group. Judy, Punch and his extensive array of spare crocodiles care of yours truly –

CORNELIA *breaks down,* VINCENT *holds her.*

CORNELIA *quickly composes herself.*

I do hope this won't put you off staying, Vincent? Because following the funeral, his wake and seven stages of grief to understand his untimely and premature death –

VINCENT. I feel sick.

CORNELIA. We owe it to him to relaunch the guesthouse. To realise his dying wish by making Vincent's a reality –

VINCENT. I can't breathe.

CORNELIA. Is that a yes? That you'll stay with me and Warren for ever? Manager?

VINCENT. I can't think about that now.

CORNELIA. I'll do your favourite tea every night –

VINCENT *breaks down, folds himself into* CORNELIA.

Only Mrs Sausage was saying, up the seven-eleven, that she's a daughter that lives in the city. Quite a popular daughter whose friends have all been dropping down like flies –

CORNELIA *clicks her fingers as:*

Just like that, Vincent.

VINCENT. Why?

CORNELIA. Rumour has it that there's too many people in your city. That it's too densely populated. And so the government have started introducing poison into the food to kill those people that society can do without.

Mrs Sausage's daughter's very well-to-do. But she does associate with a lot of lesbians and they were some of the first to go.

But she'll be back. Heidi Sausage. Give it a day or two. And she's so pretty. You'd make such a lovely local couple.

Cos it'll be gays next, she said. And then the ill. The infirm. The poor and maybe even the coloured gentlemen.

And I know you're none of those horrible things. But you have done something wrong. Otherwise you wouldn't be here.

What do you think about that?

VINCENT *sits up.*

VINCENT. I think it's rubbish.

CORNELIA. But, what if it's not?

Cos I can't lose both my boys. I can't, as a mother, think of anything worse. Anything more cruel.

I've been through enough tonight already –

RUDOLPH *appears in the hall door, holding a bottle of whiskey.*

RUDOLPH. There was a queue. Sorry.

CORNELIA. Rudolph?

VINCENT. Fucking hell –

VINCENT *launches at* RUDOLPH, *clings to him like he's going out of fashion.*

RUDOLPH. What?

VINCENT. I thought you were dead –

RUDOLPH. Hardly –

VINCENT *slaps* RUDOLPH.

VINCENT. Where the fuck have you been?

RUDOLPH. Ow –

RUDOLPH *slaps* VINCENT.

What's happening?

VINCENT *clings on to* RUDOLPH, *wrapped in relief.*

CORNELIA. I don't know.

Rudolph?

VINCENT. He's fine, Mam. Look at him. He's okay.

CORNELIA. I can see.

Oh, Rudolph, you're actually physically alive. Yeah –

CORNELIA *hugs* RUDOLPH, *a shit hug.*

RUDOLPH. I was at the seven-eleven getting Warren's whiskey. I told you. I said.

CORNELIA. Sit down, Rudolph.

RUDOLPH. What is it?

VINCENT. There's been an accident.

> CORNELIA *pulls* RUDOLPH *across to the sofa, sits him down next to her, takes his hands.*

CORNELIA. Now I don't want you to get upset, but –

RUDOLPH. Is it Matilda?

CORNELIA. It's your ice-cream van.

RUDOLPH. What about it?

VINCENT. Have you been there?

RUDOLPH. Tell me what's happened.

CORNELIA. There's been a fire. Someone's torched it.

RUDOLPH. When?

VINCENT. Just now.

CORNELIA. But they've pulled a body out.

VINCENT. We thought it was you.

CORNELIA. Who would be in your van, Rudolph?

VINCENT. If it wasn't you –

CORNELIA. I thought it was you.

> RUDOLPH *stands, paces the room, shits his pants.*

VINCENT. Well?

RUDOLPH. I don't believe you –

VINCENT. Go and see for yourself –

RUDOLPH. But how could that happen?

CORNELIA. Your guess is as good as mine –

RUDOLPH. Things don't just set ablaze like that –

CORNELIA. Apparently, someone doused the area with petrol –

VINCENT. Who was it, if it wasn't you –

RUDOLPH. I only meant to teach him a lesson.

CORNELIA. Who?

RUDOLPH. It's horrible in that van.

VINCENT. Rudolph?

RUDOLPH. No one ever comes for me.

I only wanted to keep him out the way until we were gone.

CORNELIA. Rudolph?

RUDOLPH. I locked Edward in my van.

VINCENT. Why would you do that?

RUDOLPH. Cos you were gonna go away with him and not me –

VINCENT *attacks* RUDOLPH, *they scrap like children.*

VINCENT. I hate you.

RUDOLPH. He was poison. And didn't deserve to go. But I did. He stole my chance, Vincent.

Cos I know you only came back for me. I know that.

I love you.

VINCENT. Where's Matilda?

(*Shouts, to* CORNELIA.) Where is she?

CORNELIA. Upstairs –

Exit VINCENT.

VINCENT (*off, shouts*). Matilda?

RUDOLPH. Mam?

CORNELIA. You've ruined everything.

RUDOLPH. It was you that torched it –

CORNELIA (*screams*). Only cos I thought it was you.

Enter VINCENT.

VINCENT. She's gone. She's taken all her things.

RUDOLPH. Which means we could, too –

VINCENT. She's taken Lucy.

CORNELIA. There's no need to go. No. My beautiful boys.

RUDOLPH. Mam?

CORNELIA. Because I'm your mother and I say to stay. Both of you. This is your home. And perfect now.

(*To* VINCENT.) You've nothing to go back to. There's nothing for people like us in a place like that. You've proved that. You tried, Vincent –

(*To* RUDOLPH.) And you. It's fate. Like with me and Warren. Yes.

RUDOLPH. Can I stay?

CORNELIA. I wouldn't have it any other way now.

RUDOLPH. I could run the kitchen for the guesthouse? Do starters, mains and cakes.

VINCENT. He can work spaghetti, I've seen him.

CORNELIA. First things first, they'll want to know what happened. And we have to stick together.

VINCENT. What are we gonna do?

CORNELIA. None of this ever happened. No Matilda. No Lucy. No Edward.

Hopefully, it won't have put Warren off living with us on a full-time basis. And we'll go back to having a wonderful night.

A wonderful life.

CORNELIA *pinches* VINCENT*'s cheek.*

(*To* VINCENT.) Manager.

CORNELIA *pinches* RUDOLPH*'s cheek.*

(*To* RUDOLPH.) And pastry chef.

Just one big happy family. Like when you were kids. When this guesthouse was the talk of this town. And people would line that street for just a peek inside these four walls.

Like it will be. Come here. Both. Cos –

CORNELIA *holds* RUDOLPH *on one side,* VINCENT *on the other.*

CORNELIA *smoothes down their hair with her hands as:*

Once upon a time there was a lonely crocodile that lived in the sea by a seaside town.

'Will you be my friend?' he could be heard screaming from the safe cobbled streets. But no one ever came. No one dared.

Because everybody knew that if they stepped so much as one footstep into that sea, the lonely crocodile with his empty stomach would snap them up between his angry jaws.

Until one little boy found his way home. With bigger stories about hungrier crocodiles. About lonelier ones with larger stomachs.

Crocodiles so terrifying, so menacing that not a single story would ever be needed again.

'Starships' by Nicki Minaj blares out.

MATILDA *appears in the hall door, eyes closed, recites from memory:*

MATILDA. Laura held her breath and plunged into the water. The warm hug of the sea.

She opened her eyes.

MATILDA *opens her eyes, smiles.*

Because for the first time, Laura could see perfectly. As clear as crystal, every inch of her held by the bright blue.

She never wanted to surface.

But when she did. When she eventually kicked herself free through shimmering light, the sun took each side of her face in his hands. He lathered happy kisses on it, cradled her there in the air, in his shine, in his bright yellow sparkles and blinding, dazzling hold.

Because Laura had finally become. She'd become Laura at long last.

The end.

MATILDA *exits as the lights crocodile-snap to black.*

End.

A Nick Hern Book

Crocodiles first published in Great Britain as a paperback original in 2014 by
Nick Hern Books Limited, The Glasshouse, 49a Goldhawk Road, London
W12 8QP, in association with the Royal Exchange Theatre, Manchester

Crocodiles copyright © 2014 Lee Mattinson

Lee Mattinson has asserted his right to be identified as the author of this work

Cover artwork by Moira Lam

Designed and typeset by Nick Hern Books, London
Printed in Great Britain by Mimeo Ltd, Huntingdon, Cambridgeshire PE29 6XX

A CIP catalogue record for this book is available from the British Library

ISBN 978 1 84842 443 2